FOLENS GEOGRAPHY

PEOPLE & PLACES

STEVE RICKERBY

ACKNOWLEDGEMENTS

The author and publishers would like to thank the following for permission to reproduce photographs and other material:

Cardiff Bay Development Corporation (5.2B; 5.2C; 5.3A; 5.4B; 5.4C)
Channel Tunnel Group Limited (8.5C)
Danish Tourist Board (4.5B)
Exeter City Council (9.2A)
Neil Fletcher (6.1; 6.2; 6.3)
France Image Production (5.5A)
Chas E Goad Limited, 8-12 Salisbury Square, Old Hatfield, Herts. (8.1A)
John Head (9.3A)
Lovell Urban Renewal (5.3B; 5.3C; 5.3D)
Merseyside Development Corporation (7.2A; 7.3A; 7.3B; 7.3C; 7.4D)
North Tyneside Libraries & Arts Department (1.4A)
Northern Ireland Tourist Board (4.1A)
Norwich City Council (8.1B; 8.4B)
Norwich and Norfolk Chamber of Commerce and Industry (8.2D)
Ordnance Survey (2.3A; 2.3B; 3.4F; 3.4G; 5.2A; 8.3A; 9.4A)
Robert Harding Picture Library (2.1A; 2.2B; 5.1A)
Sealink UK Limited (8.5B)
Sydney Lee (Exeter) Limited (9.2A)
Tesco Stores Limited (8.3B; 8.3C)
The Plaza, Exeter (9.2B)
Thomson Holidays Limited (9.5B)
Young Family (6.5)

Illustrators: Denby Designs
                Eric Jones
                Jillian Luff of Bitmap Graphics

Cover: Design - Tanglewood Graphics, Broadway House, The Broadway, London SW19
          Illustration - Abacus Publicity Limited

The publishers have made every effort to contact copyright holders but this has not always been possible. If any have been overlooked we will be pleased to make any necessary arrangements.

Folens books are protected by international copyright laws. All rights reserved. The copyright of all materials in this book, except where otherwise stated, remains the property of the publisher and author(s). No part of this publication may be reproduced, stored in a retrieval system, or transmitted, in any form or by any means, for whatever purpose, without the written permission of Folens Limited.

© 1990 Folens Limited, on behalf of the author.

First published 1990 by Folens Limited, Albert House, Apex Business Centre, Boscombe Road, Dunstable LU5 4RL, England.

ISBN 1 85276 081 8

Printed in Great Britain by Eagle Colour Books Limited.

CONTENTS

Unit	Title	Page
1.1	LOOKING OUT	4
1.2	INTO THE STREET	6
1.3	MOVING ABOUT	8
1.4	THEN AND NOW	10
1.5	PEOPLE AND CHANGE	12
2.1	SETTLEMENTS	14
2.2	BUCKMINSTER	16
2.3	ON THE MAP	18
2.4	LINKED SETTLEMENTS	20
2.5	DIFFERENT VILLAGES?	22
3.1	GALASHIELS	24
3.2	WHAT MAKES A TOWN?	26
3.3	ONE-WAY TRAFFIC	28
3.4	TOWNSHAPE	30
3.5	VAISON	32
4.1	BELFAST	34
4.2	BIGGER AND BIGGER	36
4.3	KEEPING CITIES IN	38
4.4	CRAIGAVON	40
4.5	COPENHAGEN	42
5.1	URBAN DECAY	44
5.2	CARDIFF DOCKS	46
5.3	WHAT'S BEING DONE?	48
5.4	THE ISSUES RAISED	50
5.5	DIEPPE	52
6.1	NEIL'S PHOTO SHOP	54
6.2	THE SHOP SYSTEM	56
6.3	LOCATING A BUSINESS	58
6.4	DIFFERENT JOBS	60
6.5	FARMING IN THE UK	62
7.1	WORKPLACES	64
7.2	MERSEYSIDE	66
7.3	BRUNSWICK BUSINESS PARK	68
7.4	WHY CHOOSE BRUNSWICK?	70
7.5	INDUSTRIES AND REGIONS	72
8.1	A CITY CENTRE - NORWICH	74
8.2	DIFFERENT SHOPS	76
8.3	OUT OF TOWN	78
8.4	SHOPPING WITHOUT SHOPS	80
8.5	ACROSS THE CHANNEL	82
9.1	LEISURE TIME	84
9.2	LEISURE IN A TOWN - EXETER	86
9.3	DARTMOOR NATIONAL PARK	88
9.4	PROTECTING THE COUNTRYSIDE	90
9.5	SUN, SEA AND SAND	92
	Glossary	94

1.1 LOOKING OUT

Target

* To understand that when you look out of a window, what you see is part of **geography**.
* To learn how to collect facts from a photograph.
* To find out what a **sketch map** is and learn how to use a **key**.

Through the window

Photo **A** is a view out of a window. It shows a street called Percy Park Road. This street is in Tynemouth, which lies on the north east coast of England.

Geography is about places and their people.

When you look out of a window, what you see is part of geography.

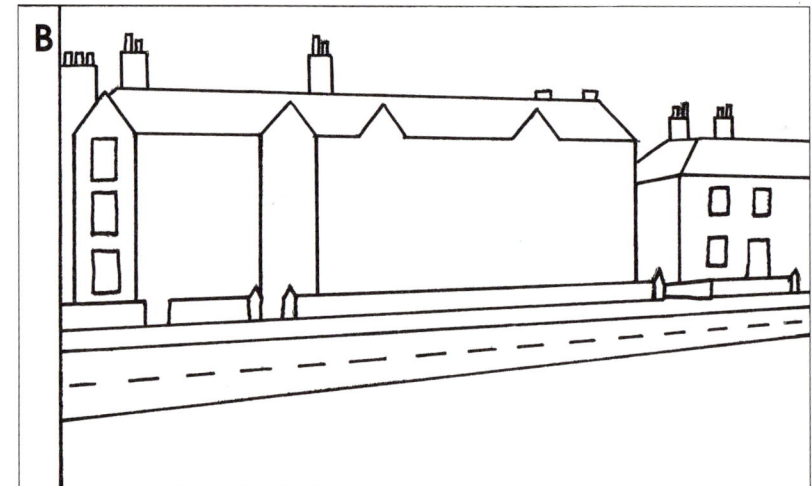
*Line sketch based upon the photo, **A***

CORE ACTIVITIES

1 Look at photo **A** and this list:
   grass tree house shop factory
   people car lorry lamp-post rain
  * Make a copy of the list.
  * Put a ring around each of the things in your list that you can see in the photo.

2 Look at **A** more closely.
  * Write down more things that you can see.
  * Try to get at least six.
  * Make a copy of this table:

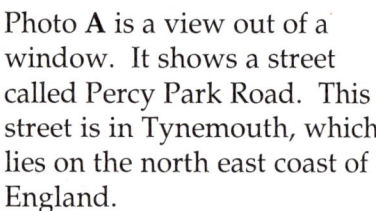

  * Find out what **street furniture** is.
    (☞ GLOSSARY)
  * Put the words you have collected from photo **A** into these lists.

3 Some of your lists may be empty.
  * Look at **A** again.
  * Try to find at least one word to put into each empty list.

4 Look at **B**. It is the start of a sketch drawn from photo **A**. You will need a copy of **B**.
  * Complete your copy of **B**, using **A** to help you.
  * Try to add at least five labels to your sketch.
    EXAMPLES: road, three-storey house.

5 **C** shows a **sketch map** of Percy Park Road.
  * Find out what a sketch map is.
    (☞ GLOSSARY)
  * Write a sentence, in your own words, to explain it.

Out of the Window

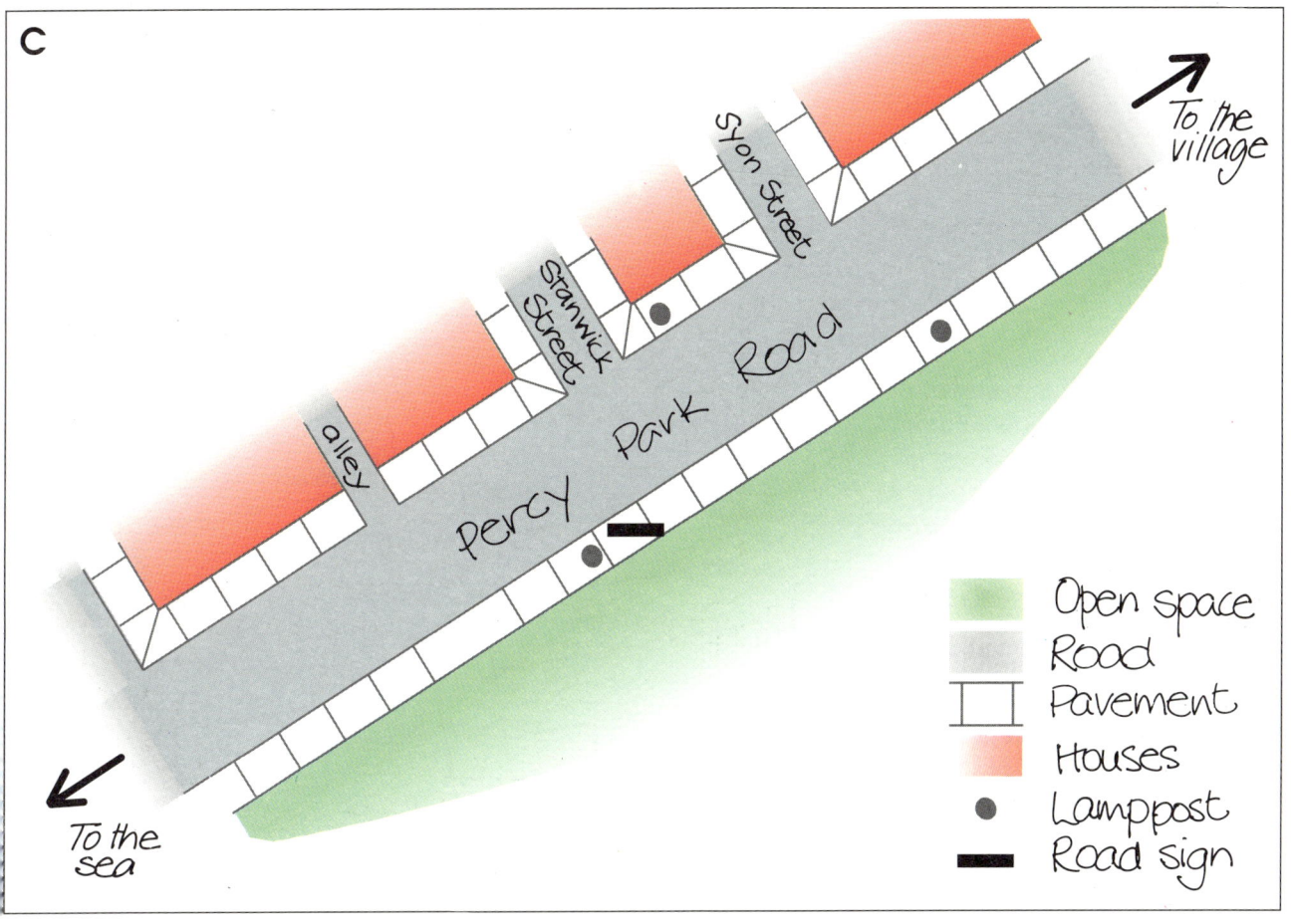

Sketch map showing part of Percy Park Road

6 Look again at **C**. It has a **key**. Keys are often on maps to explain what the **symbols** mean.
- What symbol is used to show a lamp-post?
- How is open space shown on the map?
- Describe how a road sign is shown.
- Can you think of another symbol for a road sign?
- Sketch your idea.
- Copy these sentences and say whether each one is true or false:
  - This part of Percy Park Road has houses on both sides.
  - Stanwick Street is closer to the sea than Syon Street.
  - All the side streets are on your right as you walk towards the village.
  - There is no pavement on the open space side of the street.
  - The road sign is on the left side as you walk towards the sea.

7 Look at **A** and **C** together.
- Which side of the road was the photographer standing on when he took the photo?

EXTENSION ACTIVITY

8 Look out of your window.
- Write lists of what you see using the same headings as Activity 2.
- Draw a sketch of part of what you see.
- Add some labels. Use **B** to help.
- Draw a sketch map of the view from your window.
- Give it labels, a title and a key.

1.2 INTO THE STREET

Target

* To carry out a **street survey**.
* To use a **plan**.

The view out of the window, of Percy Park Road, showed only part of the street. Buildings in another part of the street may be different. Perhaps they are used for shops instead of houses.

The best way to find this out is to go into the street and carry out a survey. A **street survey** involves collecting facts.

A shows some of the results of a street survey that was carried out in Percy Park Road. As you can see, facts for only one side of the street have been collected.

Abdul's street survey

CORE ACTIVITIES

1 Look at **A**.
   * Write down what each of these buildings is used for:
   17 21 9 23 13 1
   EXAMPLE: 17 = a chemist.

2 **B** is a photo of some of the buildings in Percy Park Road.
   * What are these buildings used for?
   * When were they built?
   * Write down at least four materials used in the buildings.
   * What numbers in the street are these buildings? (*HINT*: Use **A** to help you)

3 **C** is a **plan** and it shows what the ground floors of some of the buildings are used for. Imagine you are walking northward along Percy Park Road.
   * Carry out your own survey for the left-hand side of the street. (*HINT*: Look at **A** to see how to do this)

4 Look at **C** again.
   * Make a copy or tracing of the plan.
   * Complete your copy of the plan by adding labels. Remember, you can use **A** to find out what the buildings on the right-hand side of the street are used for.

Out of the Window

B

Buildings in Percy Park Road

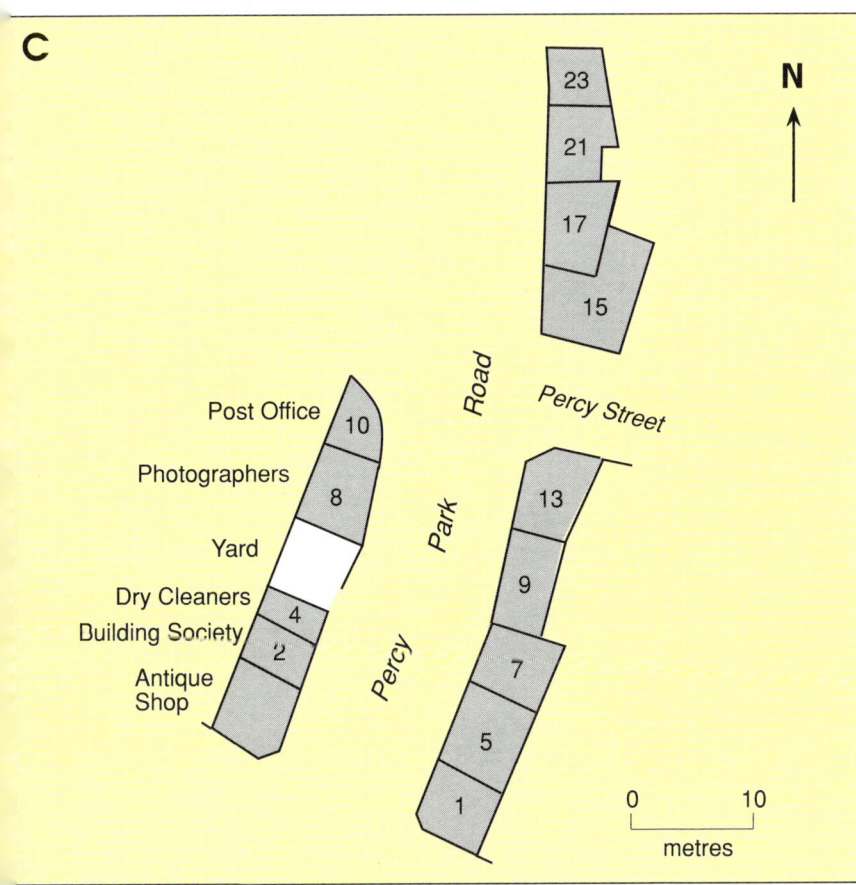

Plan of part of Percy Park Road: as it is today

Now that you have carried out your own survey for Percy Park Road, you can see that the buildings there are used for many different purposes.

EXTENSION ACTIVITIES

5 Look again at the buildings in photo **B**.
  - Make a sketch of these buildings.
  - Add labels to show as many details as you can.
    (*HINT*: **B** and **C** in Unit 1.1 will help you)

6 You might like to carry out your own street survey.
  - Find a street close to you and collect facts for it.
    You can use **A** to help you.
  - Use the facts you have collected to draw a plan.

1.3 MOVING ABOUT

Target

* To learn that the movement of people is part of geography.
* To use and make a **bar graph**.

Geography is about places. It is also about people. People make places what they are, so people are very important to geographers.

Out of the window people may be seen moving about. They may be on foot or using transport like a bicycle, a car or a bus.

A is a **bar graph** drawn from the results of a survey. The graph shows how people move along Percy Park Road, towards the village. The graph only shows a short period of time on one day.

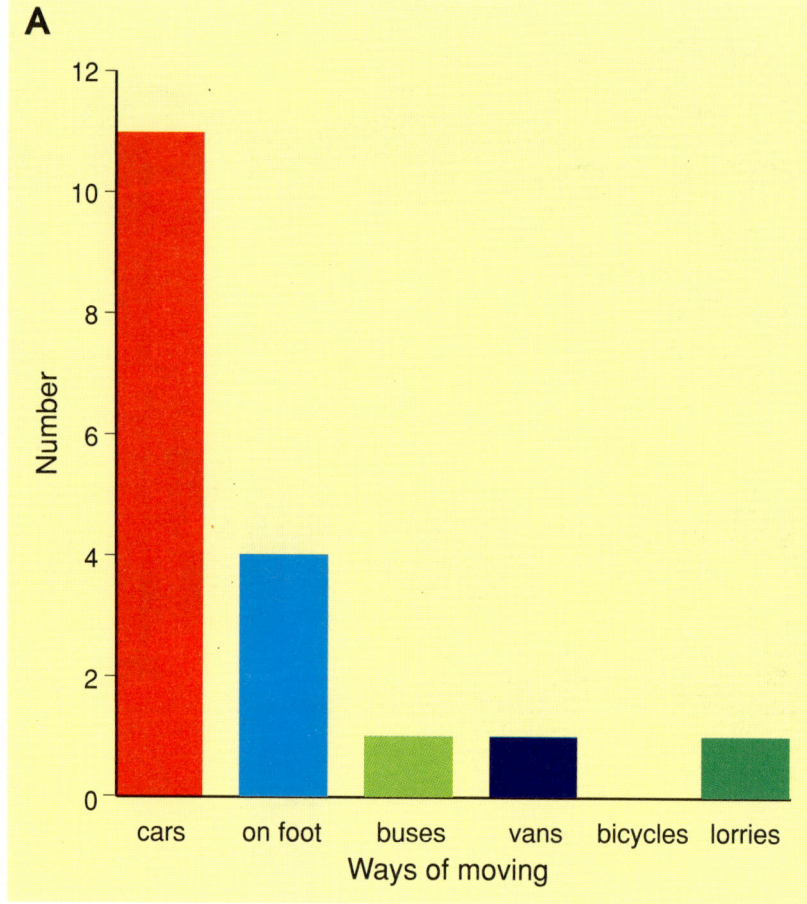

Bar graph

CORE ACTIVITIES

1 **A** tells us how many cars, walkers and so on passed the window going towards the village.
   * Make a table to show how many there were of each type. It could start like this:

TYPE OF MOVEMENT	NUMBER
By car	11

2 Use your completed table to answer these questions:
   * Which type of traffic passed most?
   * Which passed least?

3 Look at **B**. It shows different ways of moving about.
   * Write down the six different ways of moving about that it shows.

4 There are more than six ways to move about. Another six are hidden in these jumbled words:
   rtian   eraplnoae   rtomo-eikb   ihps
   epoetrlhic   heirewahlc
   * Write down what the words should be.
   EXAMPLE: rtain = train.

5 Look at **C**.
   * Use the numbers to make a bar graph similar to the one in **A**. Remember to include labels and a title.
   * Use your graph to write down the types of traffic which passed most and least often.

6 Look at **A** and at the graph you have drawn.
   * In what ways are the two graphs the same?
   * In what ways are the two graphs different?
   * Try to explain the differences you find.
   * Can you suggest reasons why the movement is greater in one direction than in the other?

Out of the Window

Different ways of moving about

C

Place	Percy Park Road	Start time	12.10
		Finish time	12.15
Direction	Towards the Sea		
Cars			12
People on foot			2
Buses			0
Vans			1
Bicycles			1
Lorries			0
Total			16

Traffic survey sheet, showing data that have been collected

EXTENSION ACTIVITIES

7 Think about a street near your home.
  - In which direction do you think most people move along it?
  - Write a sentence to answer this question.

8 You could carry out a traffic survey for your street. Perhaps it could be done from your window.
  - Collect **data** about the ways in which people move along your street, in both directions. 15 minutes is sufficient time for this.
  - Draw bar graphs to show your results.
  - In which direction do most people move?
  - Has your answer to Activity 7 been proved correct or not?
  - If it has not, try to explain why.

9

1.4 THEN AND NOW

Target

* To understand that places change.
* To use photographs and plans to collect facts about change.
* To use tables to record facts.

Places change all the time. The buildings in Percy Park Road have changed over the years. The two photos, **A** and **B**, show the village end of Percy Park Road in the 1920s and today. There have been quite a few changes.

Percy Park Road in the 1920s

CORE ACTIVITIES

1 Look at **A** and **B** very carefully. The things below belong to the Percy Park Road of either the 1920s or today:
   tram   car   zebra crossing   cafe
   lamp-post   garage   antique shop
   • Use **A** and **B** to put each of these into the correct column of a table. Your table could start like this:

1920s	TODAY

2 Using **A**:
   • Make a sketch of the old cafe building as it was in the 1920s.
   • Draw a second sketch, alongside the first, to show the cafe as it is today.
   • Compare your sketches.
   • List three things that have changed between the 1920s and today and three things that have stayed the same.

3 Look at **C**. It is a plan of building uses in 1901.
   • Draw a table to show the use of each building, on the right-hand side of Percy park Road, in 1901 and today. Unit 1.2 will help you find out what each building is used for today.
   (*HINT*: Your table will need two columns to show the uses for both 1901 and for today)

4 Use your table to answer these questions:
   • How many buildings kept the same use?
   • Which types of shop were found in this part of the street in 1901 that are still found there today?
   • There are no houses in this part of the street today. How many were there in 1901?
   • Which buildings seem to have been shops all the time?
   • What has happened to the building that was used as an hotel in 1901?

Out of the Window

Percy Park Road today

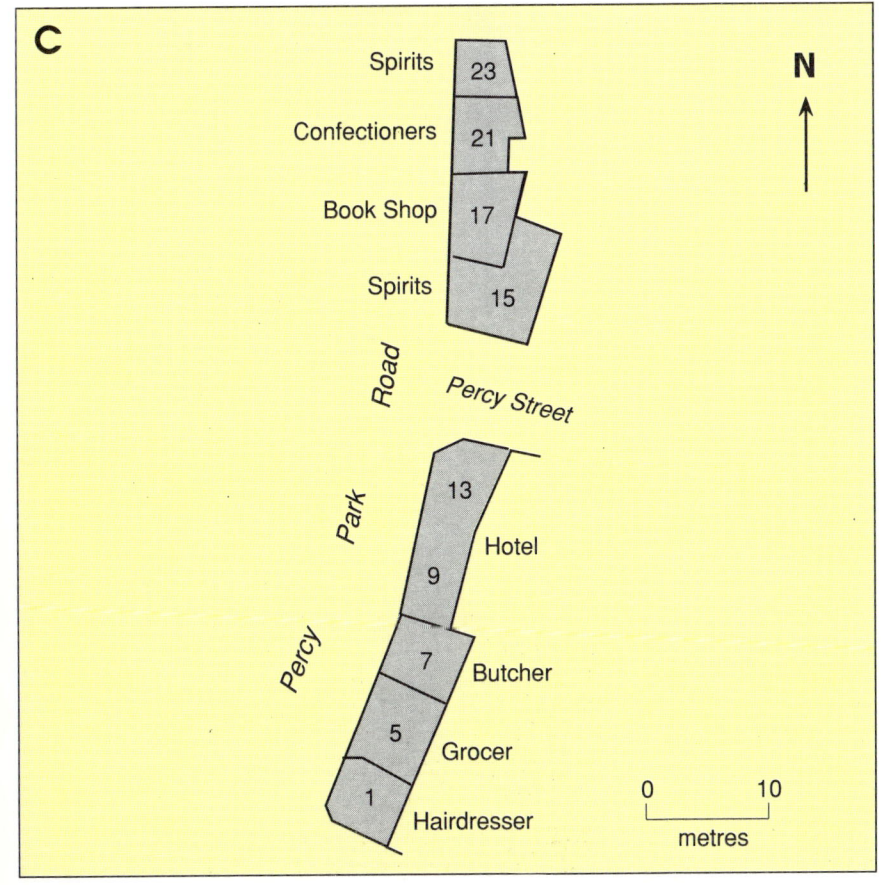

Building use plan, 1901

Most of the shops in Percy Park Road sell different things now. The plan in **C** shows how some of the buildings were used in 1901. What they sell now is shown in Unit 1.2.

EXTENSION ACTIVITY

5 Try to find out about changes in your area. You could ask older people what buildings used to be or visit the library.
- Draw a plan or sketch to show your findings, or write a report.
- You could collect newspaper cuttings and perhaps even old photos, which give information about change in your area.

1.5 PEOPLE AND CHANGE

Target

* To realise that different people may have differing views.
* To try to understand different people's views.

Parents in Tynemouth have asked the local council to make a play area for young children. It could be built on the grass triangle at the sea end of Percy Park Road (**A**).
B shows what the play area would be like.

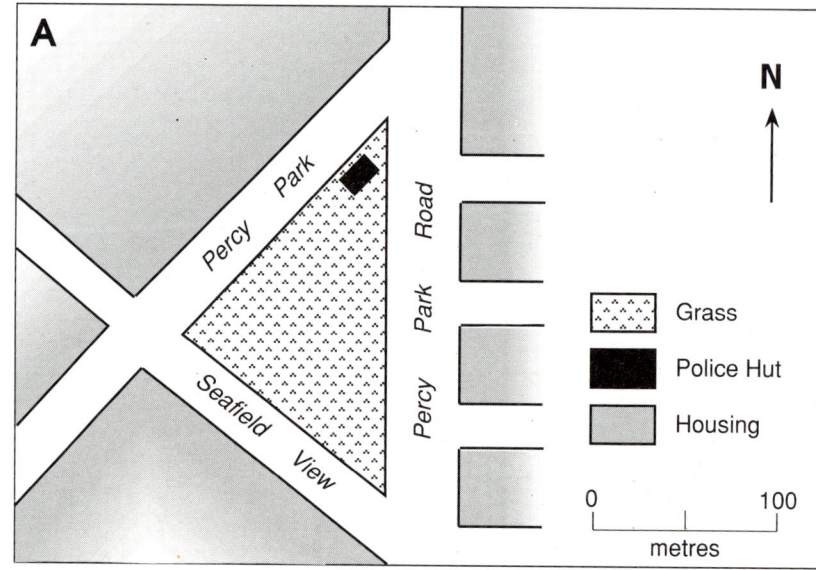

The site

The new play area

CORE ACTIVITIES

1 Look at **A**.
   - Write down the three street names.
   - Describe the position of the police hut.

2 **A** has a **scale**.
   - Measure each side of the grass triangle.
   - What is the length of each side on the plan in centimetres?
   - What is the real length of each side in metres?

3 Look at **B**.
   - Write two or three sentences to describe the new play scheme. (*HINT*: Think about what it is made of and what there is to do)

4 **C** shows the views of six people living close to where the play area would be built.
   - Read these views carefully.
   - Make two lists of views. One headed 'FOR' and the other 'AGAINST'.

Out of the Window

C

Views about the scheme

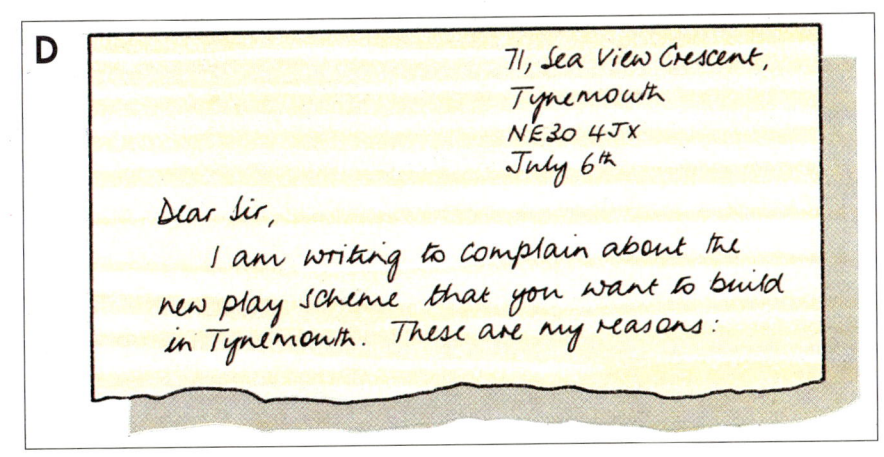

D

71, Sea View Crescent,
Tynemouth
NE30 4JX
July 6th

Dear Sir,
 I am writing to complain about the new play scheme that you want to build in Tynemouth. These are my reasons:

Bill's letter

When changes are likely, people often disagree about them. This makes the change an **issue** and people take sides (**C**). Bill objects so much that he has written to the local council.

EXTENSION ACTIVITY

5 Read **D**. Bill has decided to write a letter to the council.
• Read what he has written and finish his letter to the council. (*HINT*: Read the people's views again (**C**))
• Write your own letter to back the council's scheme.

6 Think about both sets of views.
• Do you think either side is right?
• Explain your answer.

7 Television often deals with issues.
• Imagine a TV interview between a presenter and two of the people shown in **C**.
• Write out how the interview might go. It might start like this:
Presenter: *"Good morning. Today we have two people from Tynemouth to talk about a new play area. Let me introduce them. First there is... "*

2.1 SETTLEMENTS

Target

* To understand that **settlements** are places where people live.
* To learn that settlements can be different sizes.

A village - an example of a small settlement

Settlements are places where people live. There are settlements of all sizes.

Hamlet and **village** are names used to describe small settlements. **Town, city** and **conurbation** describe large settlements.

A and **B** are photos showing two types of settlement but there are quite a few more, as **C** shows.

A town - an example of a large settlement

CORE ACTIVITIES

1 Here are some words and phrases about settlements:
  quiet   busy   market   many shops
  lots of traffic   countryside   cinema
  few people   bus station   hospital
  * Decide which words and phrases you think are to do with a village and which are to do with towns.
  * Make two lists out of these words. One with the title 'VILLAGE' and the other with the title 'TOWN'.

2 Look at **A** and **B** again.
  * Find out what village and town mean.
    (☞ GLOSSARY)
  * What makes the place in **A** look like a village?
  * What can you see in **B** that makes this place look like a town?

3 **C** is a sketch of five different settlements. Each one is shown by a letter.
  * Copy out each of the following descriptions and say which letter it matches. The first one has been done for you.
  Farmstead - the smallest type of settlement. Letter = C.
  Village - small settlement with a church and usually just a few shops.
  Town - bigger than a village with more shops and maybe some factories.
  Hamlet - very small with just a few houses.
  City - a big settlement with many shops and tall buildings.

4 Think about where you live.
  * Say what sort of settlement you think it is and explain why.

14

A Place to Live

Settlement types

EXTENSION ACTIVITIES

5 Think of the names of settlements you have been to or know about. It could be a long list.
- Draw a table like the one shown here:

| SETTLEMENT NAME | SETTLEMENT TYPE |
|---|---|//

- Write under 'SETTLEMENT NAME' all the places you have thought of.
- Now write next to them in the column 'SETTLEMENT TYPE', what you think each one is.

6 Really big British cities are sometimes called conurbations
- Find out what this word means, and the names of some conurbations.
- Make a map to show where they are.

15

2.2 BUCKMINSTER

Target

* To understand that villages provide a range of **services**.
* To use a sketch map to give directions.

The village shop

A typical village pub

Buckminster is a village. In Buckminster, there are houses but there are also other buildings, including shops, a post office and a garage. Some of these buildings are shown by the photos on these pages.

These other buildings provide **services** for the people who live in the village. People who live in smaller settlements nearby, such as farms, visit the village to use its services.

CORE ACTIVITIES

1 Here is a fuller list of the services in Buckminster: shops (grocer, confectioner, chemist, greengrocer, stationer, antiques)   Post Office   garage   pub serving drinks and food
  * Look up any of these words that you do not know in a dictionary.
  * Look at **A**. Write down four things that the shop sells.

2 **D** is a sketch map of Buckminster.
  * Make a copy of this map.
  * On your copy, label the shop, the pub and the antique shop by using these clues to help you:
    - The shop is the small building standing on its own at the south end of Cow Row.
    - The pub is the last building on the east side of the main street before you turn right towards Colsterworth.
    - The antique shop is at the north end of Cow Row.

3 Imagine you are an elderly person living in Buckminster.
  * Which service would you use if you wanted:
    - to buy a sandwich
    - to have a cup of coffee
    - to fill your car up with petrol
    - to buy a stamp
    - to meet a friend for lunch
    - to collect your pension
    EXAMPLE: I would use the village shop to buy a sandwich.
  * Which of the services are you least likely to use?
  * Explain why.

4 Look at **D** again.
  * Give directions from the shop to each of these places:
    - the pub
    - the antique shop
    - the road that leads to the A1
    - Sewstern

A Place to Live

C

Buckminster antiques

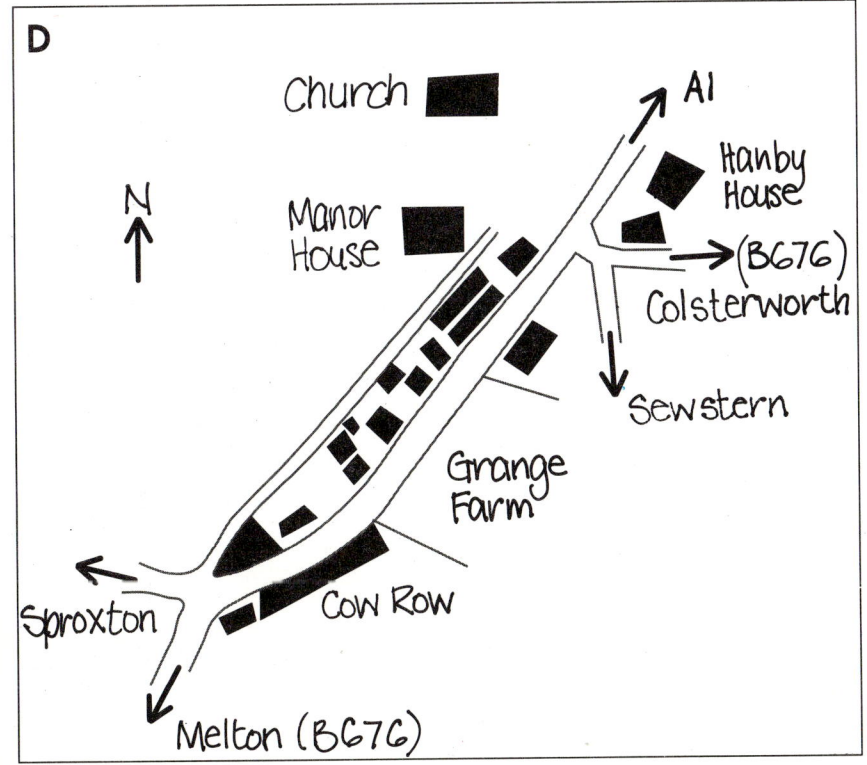

Sketch map of Buckminster village

EXTENSION ACTIVITIES

5 Think about how often you would use each service if you lived in Buckminster.
  ● Would you use each service daily, weekly or not often?
  ● Present your choices in a table like this:

DAILY	WEEKLY	NOT OFTEN

  ● Count how many services there are in each column and make a bar graph to show your results.
  ● Write a short description of what your graph shows.

6 Repeat Activity 5 for a village or street you know.

2.3 ON THE MAP

Target

* To be able to use the symbols and **grid** on **Ordnance Survey maps**.

In geography you will often use **Ordnance Survey maps**. These are detailed **maps** which show even the smallest settlement. Every place in Great Britain appears on Ordnance Survey maps. **A** shows part of an Ordnance Survey map on which Buckminster is marked.

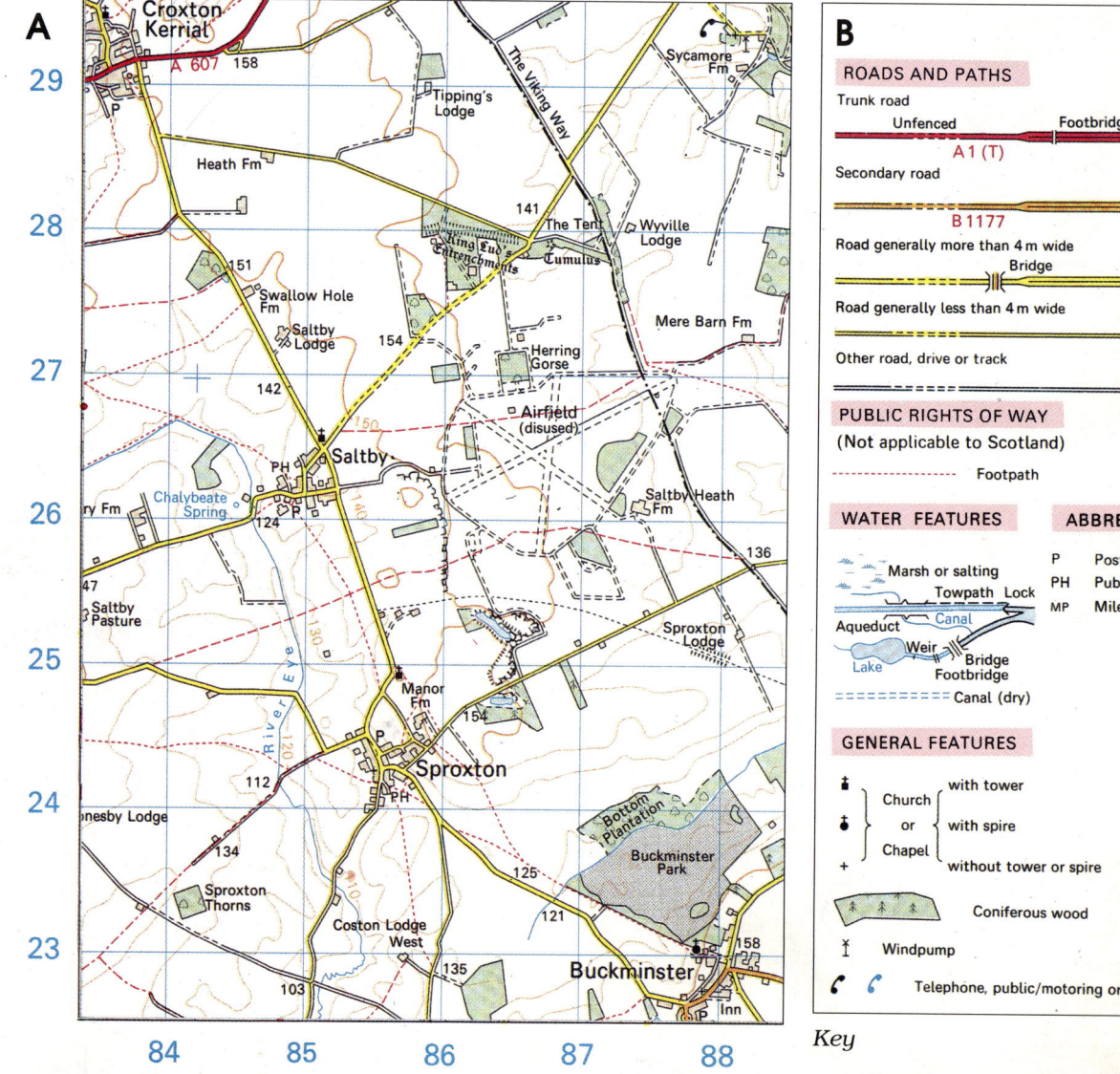

1:50 000 Ordnance Survey map extract

CORE ACTIVITIES

1 Look at the map (**A**).
- Find the village of Buckminster.
- Here are the names of three other villages on the map. The letters in their names have been jumbled up:
  xonoStpr   noroCxt   ielrrKa   baytSl
- Rearrange the letters to spell their correct names.

2 Farms are shown on the map.
- List five of them. (HINT: Fm. = farm)

3 **B** shows symbols used on the map.
- Draw these symbols:
  main road   footpath   telephone   lake
  coniferous wood   church with tower
  windpump   Post Office   public house

A Place to Live

All Ordnance Survey (O.S.) maps have a key to show what the symbols on the map mean.

B is part of an O.S. map key. It explains some of the important symbols found on map **A**.

Map **A** has blue squares drawn over it. These squares form a **grid**.

Grid squares can be used to help describe where a place is on the map. **C** shows how.

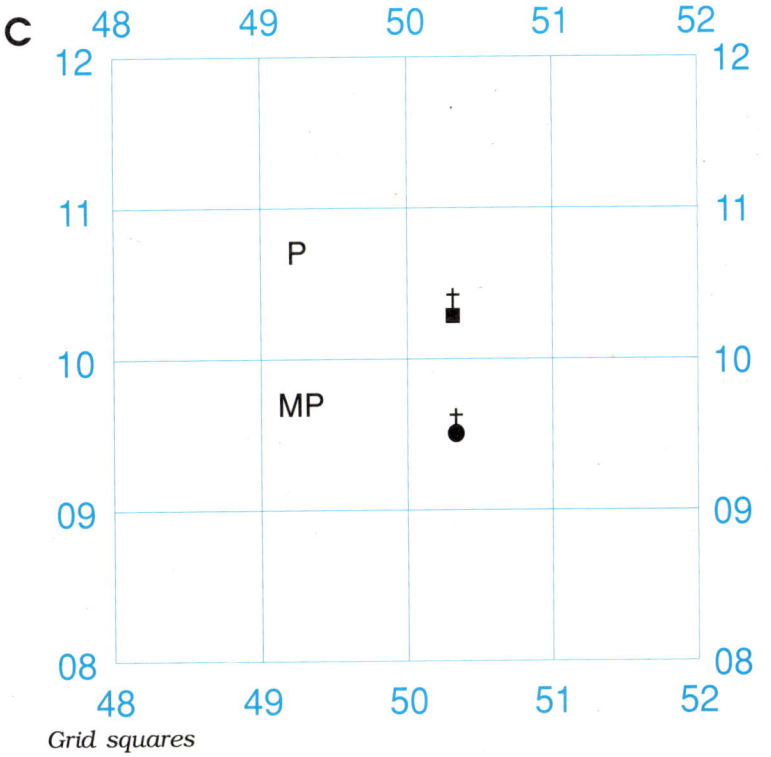

Grid squares

4 Colours on the map have special meanings.
- This list of colours and meanings is wrong:
  green = water
  blue = **trunk road**
  yellow = wood
  red = secondary road
  orange = minor road
- Match each colour with its correct meaning.
  EXAMPLE: red = secondary road

5 Look carefully at Buckminster. The map tells you facts about the village using symbols.
- With the help of **B** copy and complete this description. Choose your answers from the list at the end.
  Buckminster has a _____ road and three _____ roads.
  There is an ___ and a ____ _____ .
  There is a church with a _____ and a small _____ .
  inn   spire   chapel   Post Office   minor   secondary
- Write your own descriptions for the other three villages.

6 Copy **C**.
- Write sentences to give the **grid references** of the Post Office, the church with tower, the milepost and the church with spire. The reference for the Post Office has been given for you.
- Use **A** to write down grid references for the following:
  - Saltby Post Office
  - Croxton Kerrial church
  - Sproxton's public house
  - the pond near Buckminster
  - Saltby Heath Farm

The Post Office is in square 4910.
Look at where the 49 and 10 lines cross.

49 is the EASTING.
It comes first.
10 is the NORTHING.
It comes second.

The GRID REFERENCE is 4910.

EXTENSION ACTIVITY

7 Find another O.S. map which shows village settlements.
- Using Activities 5 and 6 as a guide, write descriptions of three villages from this map.
- Practice giving grid references by writing down grid references for ten named farms on your map.

2.4 LINKED SETTLEMENTS

Target

* To understand that settlements can be linked together.
* To understand that **links**, like roads, allow people to go to other settlements to use their services.
* To see how transport links between settlements can become an issue.

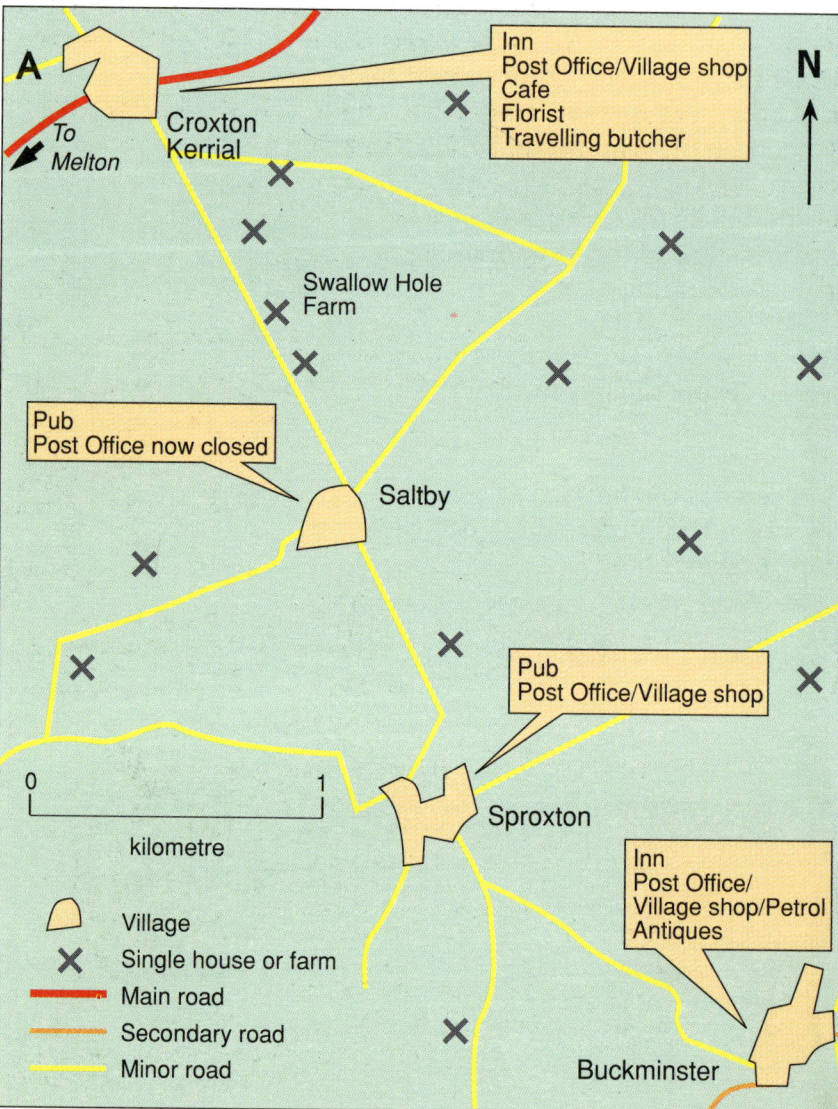

Settlement pattern

A shows Buckminster and three other Leicestershire villages. Leicestershire is the English county where they are located.

Each village is linked to its neighbours by road (**A**). Map **A** also shows the locations of smaller settlements surrounding the villages as well as the services each settlement has.

People may have to travel between settlements for services.

CORE ACTIVITIES

1 Answer these questions:
* How many villages are there on the map?
* Which is the only village on a main road?
* How many single houses and farms are shown?
* Which village is furthest south?
* How many roads lead out of Saltby?

2

VILLAGE	SERVICES	ROADS
Saltby	Post Office, pub.	4 minor roads

* Make a copy of this table.
* Complete the table by filling in details for the other three villages.

3 Croxton Kerrial has the most services.
* Give a reason for this.

4 Imagine setting off from Swallow Hole Farm (**A**) to buy the things on this list:
  petrol stamps flowers bread cheese fruit
* Write a description of your shopping trip saying where you would buy each item. You should travel the shortest distance you can.
* How many villages would you have to visit?

5 Read the comments people make in **C**.
* What three reasons do the people give for wanting to go to Melton?
* Other people get to Melton without using the bus. How?
* Why are there fewer buses now than years ago?
* Why can the bus company not put more services on?

A Place to Live

Buckminster is connected to some of its neighbouring settlements by bus. **B** shows the timetable of one of the two buses that serve Buckminster. Melton is the nearest town.

In the countryside some people rely on buses to do their weekly shopping in the nearest town. Catching the bus is not always as easy as it is in a city. The people in **C** explain why this is an issue for them.

B

ROUTE 10

SEWSTERN TO MELTON

	Tues	
Sewstern	0930	1300
Buckminster	0935	1305
Sproxton	-	1311
Saltby	-	1316
Stonesby	-	1321
Croxton Kerrial	-	-
Saxby	0947	-
Melton	1000	1340

MELTON TO SEWSTERN

Melton	0900	1215
Saxby	0913	1228
Croxton Kerrial	-	-
Stonesby	-	-
Saltby	-	-
Sproxton	-	-
Buckminster	0925	1240
Sewstern	0930	1245

Bus timetable

The country bus issue

6 Tuesday is market day in Melton. You live in Buckminster and want to go to the market.
- Use **B** to help you choose the correct ending for each of these sentences about your bus journey there.
  - The number of the bus is (2 4 10 23).
  - The time the early bus leaves Buckminster is (0935 1305 0925).
  - You will arrive in Melton at (0947 1215 1000).
  - Your journey will have taken (25 30 35) minutes.
  - You can catch the bus back from Melton at (1000 1215 1305).
  - The bus is due to arrive back in Buckminster at (1240 1245 1305).

EXTENSION ACTIVITIES

7 Think about your own use of services.
- What do you have to travel to buy or to do?
- Where do you go?
- How do you get there?
- Is it easy to make the journey?
- What problems are there?
- Write a few sentences to explain these things.

8 Imagine you live in Buckminster. You think there should be more buses.
- Design a poster to advertise a village meeting to discuss the issue. Your poster needs to be eye-catching. It should say clearly why more buses are needed.

2.5 DIFFERENT VILLAGES?

Target

* To compare two villages.
* To test ideas by scoring.

Villages are found in every country, but just how different are they? To try to find out you are going to compare Buckminster with the village shown in **A**. This village is called Crestet and it is in the south of France. **B** gives some facts about Crestet and its **location**.

A

A village in France

CORE ACTIVITIES

1 Look carefully at **A**.
   • Make an outline sketch of it.
   • Draw and label these features:
      hilltop   village   steep slope
      woods   telephone wire   church

2 Look at **B**.
   • Read the following statements. Some are true and others are false.
      - Vaison is south of Crestet.
      - The restaurants are close to the main road.
      - The old village is over 300 metres above sea-level.
      - Fewer than 200 people live in the village.
      - In straight line, the old village is about 1 kilometre from the main road.
   • Copy out those statements which you think are true.
   • Correct those statements which you think are false.

3 The table (**C**) gives some facts about Buckminster and Crestet.
   • Make a copy of **C**.
   • Now fill in the empty boxes. To do this, collect facts about Buckminster from Unit 2.2. Use **B** to gather facts about Crestet.

4 This table will also let you compare the two villages and test how different they really are.
   • Copy out the list of side headings from **C** again.
   • For each heading, decide how different the two villages are.
   • Next to each heading write a score of 1 if you think the two villages are exactly the same, a score of 2 if they are slightly different and 3 if they are very different.
   • Now add the scores. (The higher your score, the bigger the difference.)
   • What is the highest score you could possibly have?
   • Write down your score and a sentence to say if it shows the villages are the same, slightly different or very different.

22

A Place to Live

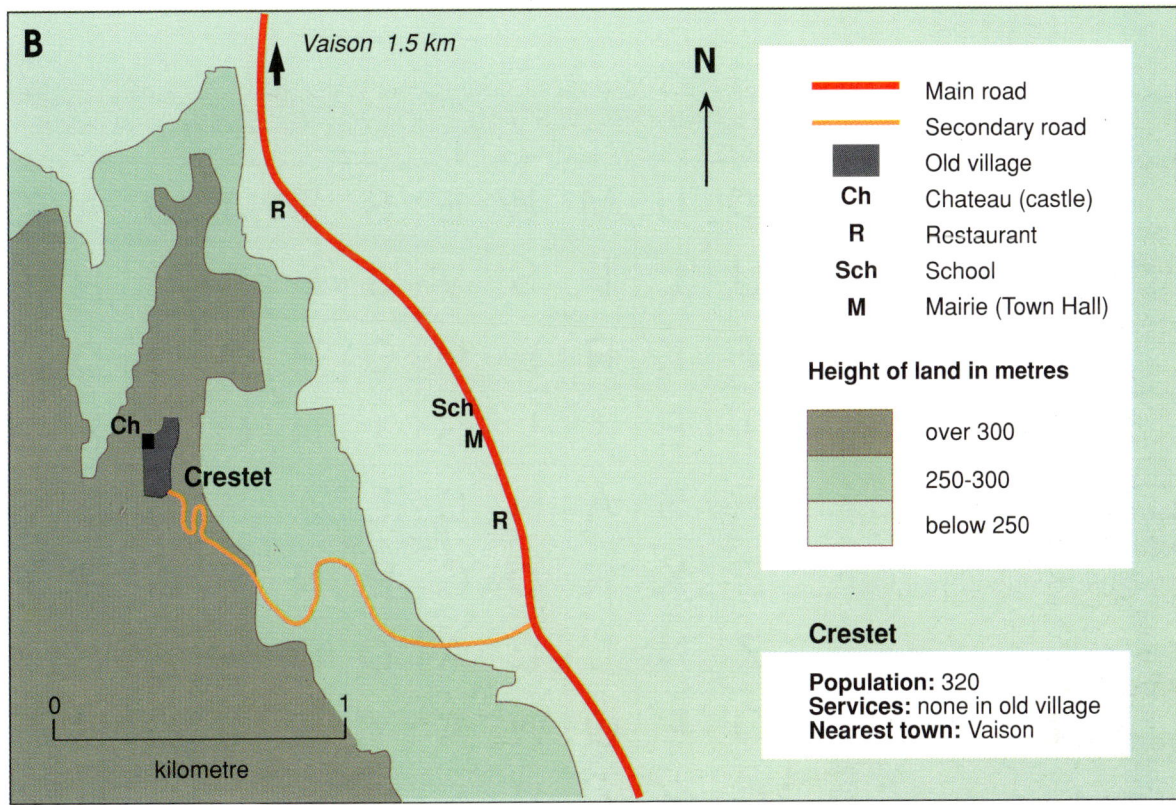

Crestet

C

Village name	BUCKMINSTER	Crestet
Services		None in the old village. 2 restaurants on the main road
Local town	Melton (15 kilometres away)	
Buses		1 to Vaison
Road links		1 secondary road leading to main road

Comparing villages

EXTENSION ACTIVITIES

5 Read these sentences and decide which you think true. (You may decide on more than one):
 - Crestet has fewer services because it is closer to its local town.
 - Crestet's restaurants are close to the main road because it is busy.
 - Buckminster has more shops because it has more roads.
 • Copy out the sentences that you think are true.

6 Being close to a main road or being close to a town may affect the number of services a village has.
 • Try to think of something else that might affect the number of services a village has.
 • Explain the effect this might have - will it mean more or fewer services?

7 Use the method you have learned in this unit to compare more villages with Buckminster and Crestet. You could choose the villages in Unit 2.4 or a village you know about.

23

3.1 GALASHIELS

Target

* To take information from a photograph.
* To use an atlas to find place names.
* To learn the names of some places in Scotland.

Galashiels is a town in the south east of Scotland. It is in the Borders Region about 56 kilometres from Edinburgh. Edinburgh is Scotland's capital city.
You can see the exact location of Galashiels on the map, **C**.

A

Welcome to Galashiels

B

D	U	M	W	E	S	T	T	B	A	G
U	L	F	S	V	J	E	A	O	R	E
F	K	R	E	H	C	R	Y	S	D	O
I	E	I	L	S	I	N	O	I	E	R
F	S	A	N	D	L	A	R	D	E	S
E	K	R	O	G	E	N	T	W	B	F
Z	N	L	L	A	C	D	N	A	L	X
O	E	O	W	A	Y	E	I	G	H	F
G	Y	L	E	L	Y	D	H	A	N	D
H	I	A	N	C	Z	E	T	L	P	M
T	O	L	T	H	T	H	N	A	I	A
S	T	R	A	P	H	S	H	R	G	R

Scotland's regions

CORE ACTIVITIES

1 Look at **A**.
 * Complete this description by using words from the list at the end.
   The sign welcomes people to _____ which is a ____ in _____. It looks as though the photo was taken at ____. Signs like this are found at the ____ of towns.
   Edinburgh France Scotland centre Galashiels town edge midday village evening
 * Draw a sketch of the sign in **A**.
 * Label these things:
   - the Scottish flag
   - the town crest
   - the flower bed

2 You will need a copy of **C** and an atlas.
 * Find a map of Scotland in the atlas.
 * Use it to complete the sea names on a copy of **C**.

3 There are some big towns and cities on the map in **C**. These are shown by red dots.
 * Use your atlas to help you name them.

4 Scotland is made up of twelve regions. Their names are hidden in the puzzle in **B**. Borders has been done for you.
 * Find the names of the other eleven.
 * Colour each region on your map, using different colours, and write its name in the correct place.

24

In the Town

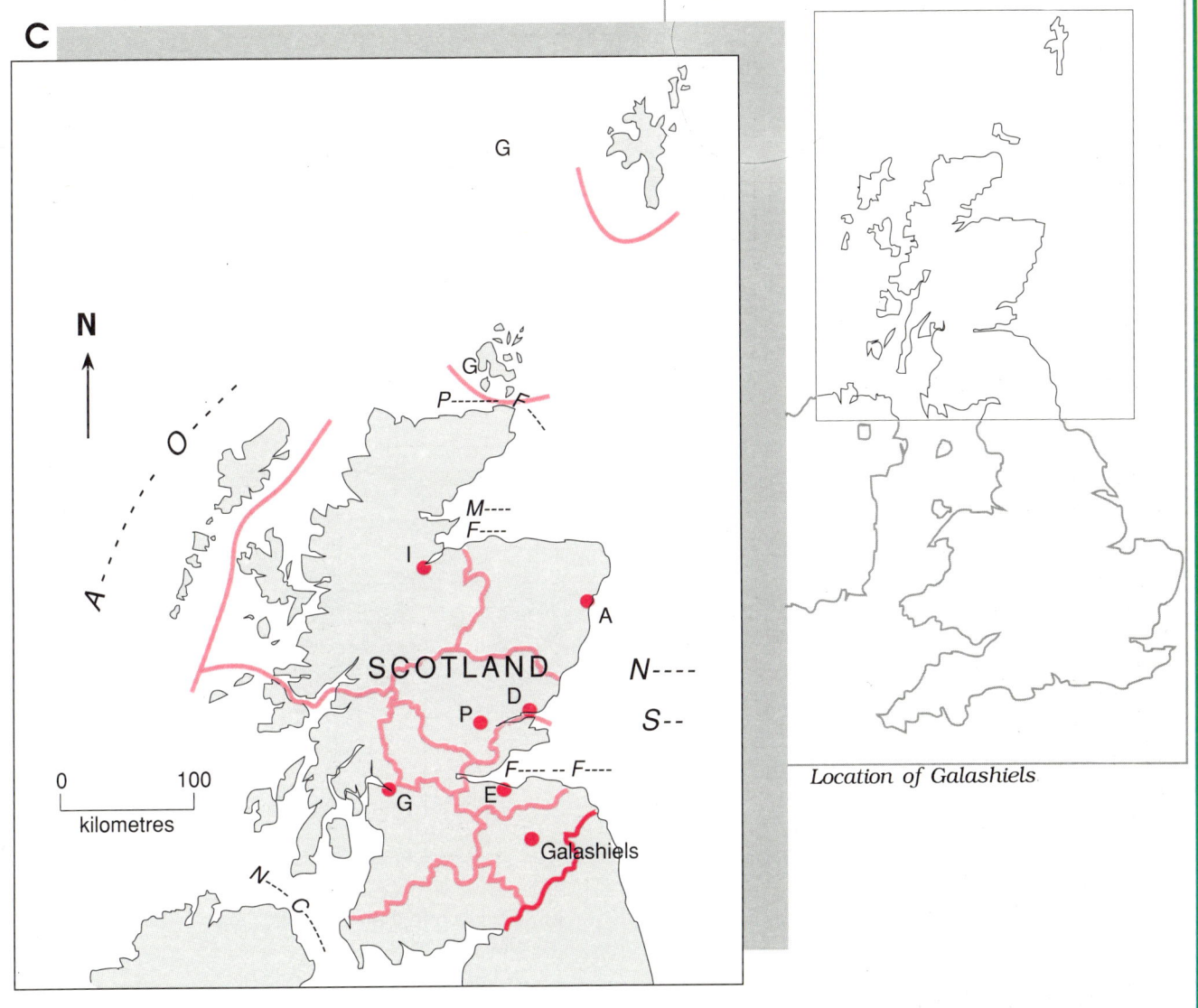

Location of Galashiels

EXTENSION ACTIVITIES

5 Think about the Welcome to Galashiels sign (**A**).
- How does it make the town seem attractive to people?
- Try to list three things.
- Now design a sign for a town you know.

6 Think about the region names.
- Try to explain some of these.
EXAMPLE: Strathclyde is named after the River Clyde.

7 The location of Galashiels is described in this unit as south east Scotland.
- Using an atlas, find the place where you live.
- Describe the location of it.

3.2 WHAT MAKES A TOWN?

Target

* To understand that towns offer more services than villages.
* To use a street map.
* To use a **tally chart** to make a graph.
* To learn what an **hypothesis** is and how to test it.

Towns are usually bigger than villages. Towns usually have more people than villages. What really makes a place a town though is what services it offers. Towns offer more services than villages.
B is a **tally chart** and gives facts about the services in Channel Street which is the busiest shopping street in Galashiels. The street map (**A**) shows part of the town, including Channel Street.

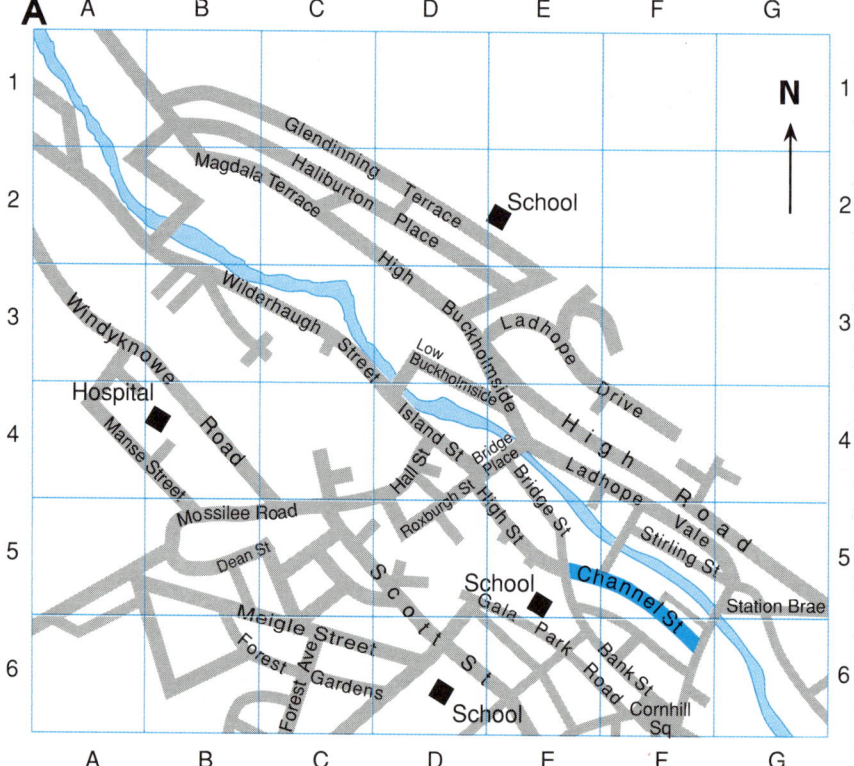

Street map of Galashiels

CORE ACTIVITIES

1 Find Channel Street on **A**. It is mostly in square F5.
   • Write down a street name found in each of these squares:
   C6   B5   G5   F5   E3   F6
   • Which squares are the three schools found in?

2 Below are two lists. One list shows places on the street map and the other shows grid squares:
   Station Brae   E4
   Island Street   B2
   Dean Street   D4
   Bridge Street   G5
   Magdala Terrace   B5
   • Match each place with its correct square.

3 If you walked to the hospital from Channel Street which way would you go?
   • Write a list of the streets you would walk along.
   • Do the same for a journey between the hospital and the school in square E2.

4 Look at **B**. It shows the numbers of different shops and services in Channel Street.
   • Use it to complete the following:
   - wool shops =
   - department stores =
   - food shops =
   - empty buildings =
   - other services =
   - shoe shops =
   • Draw a bar graph to show these data.
   • Write a sentence to describe the graph.

5 Look at **D**.
   • Write a description of what you see using these words:
   green   flat   modern   station   people

6 Study **C**.
   • Use it to make a list of the places that Galashiels buses run to.
   • Write down how far it is to each place from Galashiels. Use the scale to help you.

In the Town

Shops	Other Services	Empty
Newsagents II	Post Office I	II
Jewellers I	Bank I	
Shoes IIII	Pubs I	
Wool IIII	Building Society III	
Travel Agents I	Hotel I	
Electricals II	Insurance offices I	
Photos I		
Cleaners I		
Sports I		
Clothes II		
Cards I		
Bakers I		
Furniture I		
Chemist I		
Leather goods I		
Department stores III		

Services in Channel Street - how do these differ from those in Buckminster (Unit 2.2)?

B People from surrounding villages visit towns to make use of the services on offer there. Many people travel into Galashiels by bus and **C** shows places that buses from Galashiels bus station (**D**) go to.

Galashiels bus station

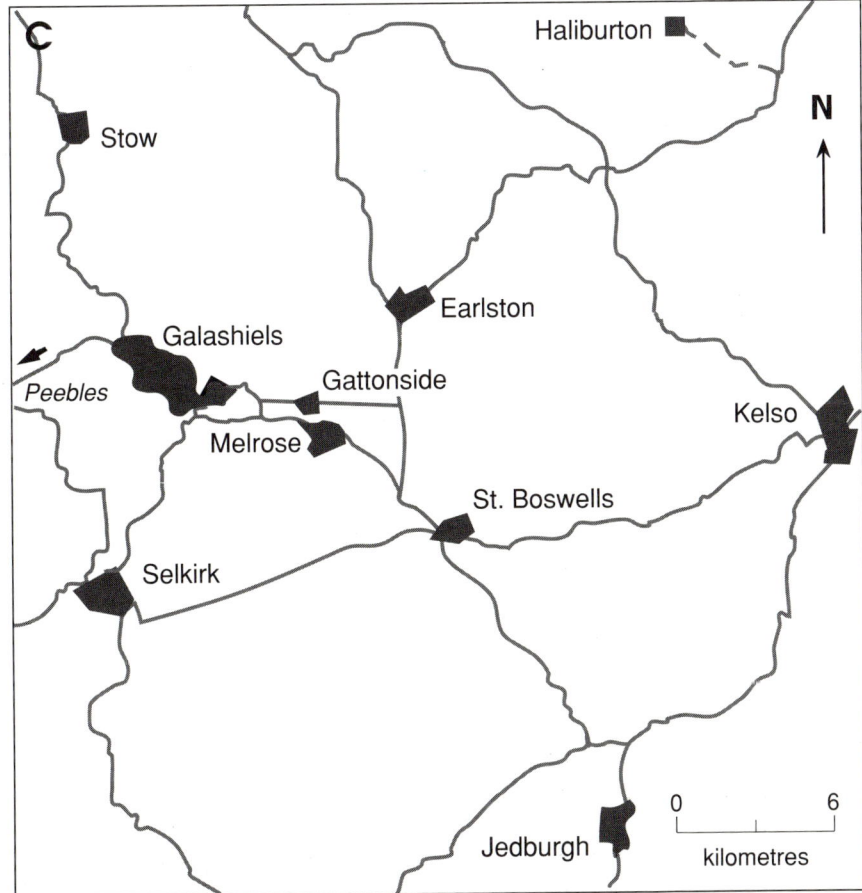

Galashiels bus links

EXTENSION ACTIVITIES

7 Read this statement:
"Buses from Galashiels mostly go to places that are within 6 kilometres of the town."
This statement is really just an idea but it can be tested to find out whether it is true or not. An idea like this is called an **hypothesis**.
Is it true or not? Follow these steps to find out.
- On a copy of **C** draw circles, or part circles, to show distances of 3, 6, 9, 12 kilometres from Galashiels.
- Count how many places there are within each circle.
- Put your data in a table.
- Make a graph to present your results.
- Write a conclusion to say if the hypothesis is true or not.

8 Your data are not enough to decide how far most buses go.
- Explain why not and say what extra data you would need to find out.

3.3 ONE-WAY TRAFFIC

Target

* To learn about **one-way traffic systems**.
* To understand that one-way systems can become an issue.
* To practice map skills.

Traffic is a problem in many town centres. Too much traffic blocks the streets and causes traffic jams. This leads to delays for motorists and it creates a great deal of noise and unpleasant fumes. It can also cause accidents.

Some towns try to solve problems like this by creating a **one-way traffic system**. Think about the town you live in, or one close to where you live; does it have a one-way system?

If you look at **A**, you will see that Galashiels has a one-way system of streets.

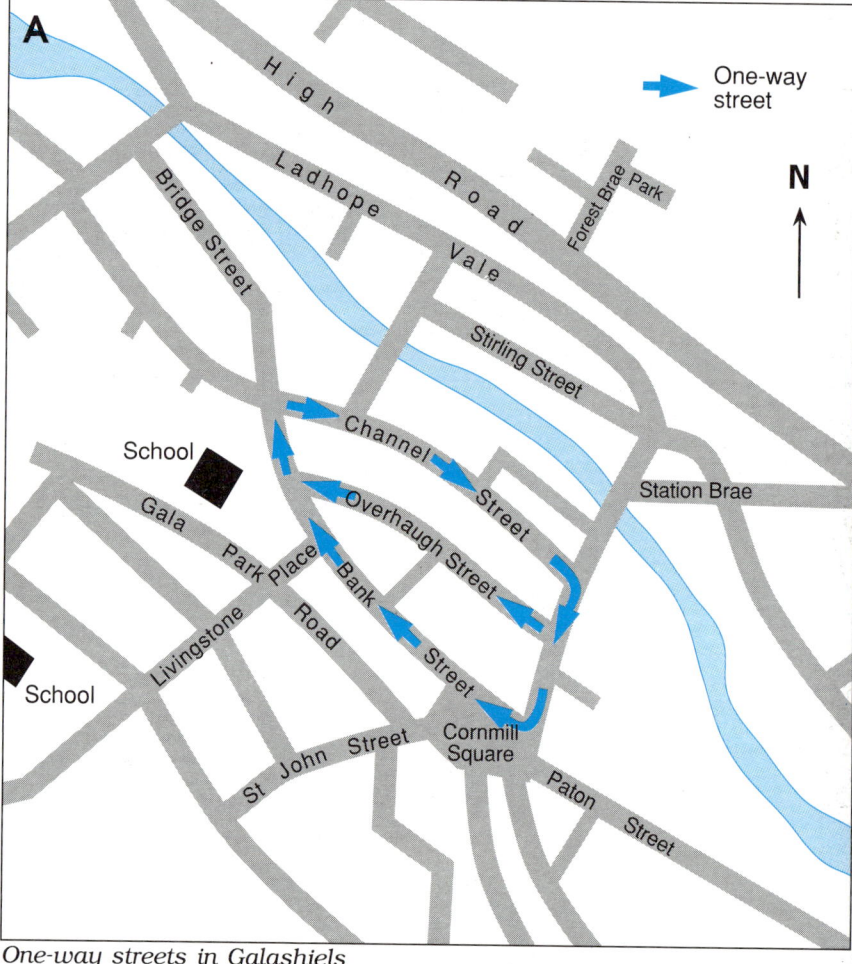

One-way streets in Galashiels

CORE ACTIVITIES

1 Look at **A**. You are in a car going north west along Paton Street. You want to reach Station Brae.
 * Describe the way the car has to go to get to Station Brae.
 * Which way would you go if you were walking?
 * Which way is shorter, in distance?
 * Give directions to motorists between these places:
   - Forest Brae and the school on Gala Park Road
   - Bridge Street and St John Street

2 **B** shows some traffic problems that are often found in towns and other large settlements.
 * Make a list of the problems you can see in the sketch.
 * Does this part of town have a one-way system?
 * How can you tell?

3 **B** shows some views about one-way streets.
 * Read these carefully.
 * Make a list of the views which are against one-way streets and another to show those views in favour of one-way streets.
 * Write down those views which are about:
   - keeping the traffic moving
   - safety
   - finding the way
 * What do you think of one-way streets? Are they a good idea?
 * Explain your answer.

4 **C** is a photo showing part of Galashiels' one-way system.
 * How is the traffic flow here made easier compared with the traffic flow shown in **B**?

In the Town

One-way streets are not liked by everyone. They are meant to help solve the traffic problems of towns. Some people, though, have other ideas about how to stop traffic jams and keep the streets safe for pedestrians.

Traffic problems, then, are an issue in towns.

Views about one-way streets

Part of the one-way system in Galashiels

EXTENSION ACTIVITY

5 You are a T.V. news reporter. You have been asked to go to both Galashiels and the town shown in **B** and prepare a report, comparing the traffic conditions between the two places.
- Write a script for your report.
- Put what you will say and include interviews with these people:
  - a traffic planner
  - a parent of a young child
  - a lorry driver

29

3.4 TOWNSHAPE

Target

* To understand that the shape of a town can be due to the shape of the land.
* To understand how towns are made up of **land-use zones**.
* To find the height of the land from an O.S. map.
* To read a land-use map.

In towns like Galashiels, different parts of the land are used in different ways. Due to this, the town can be split into **land-use zones**. These land-use zones make a pattern.

A shows the pattern of land-use in part of Galashiels. It shows zones of the town. In each zone one type of land use is most important.

The photos, **B** to **E**, show different zones in Galashiels. **E** shows more than one zone.

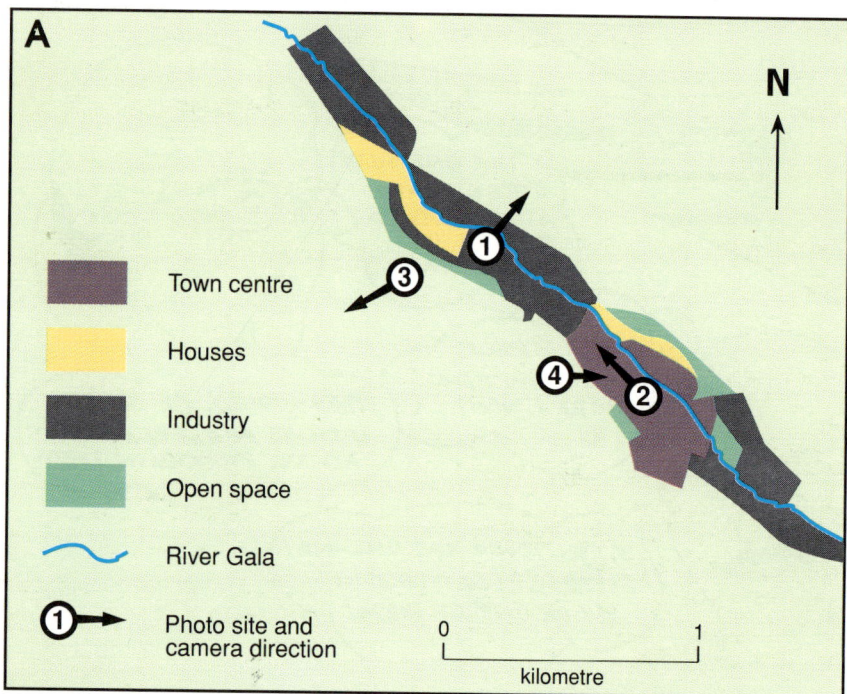

Land-use in Galashiels. How would you describe the shape of the town?

Central Business District

Residential zone

CORE ACTIVITIES

1 Look at **A**.
  • Make a list of the four land-use zones shown.

2 Some of the following statements are true and others are false.
  - Houses cover the most space.
  - Most industry is along the river.
  - All the open space is together.
  - The town centre is more than 1 kilometre across.
  - The north west of Galashiels is mostly housing.
  • Copy out each statement and say whether it is true or false.

3 Look at **A** and at the photos. **A** has numbers, 1 to 4, written on it to show the exact site where each photo was taken.
  • Match up the site numbers with the photo letters. EXAMPLE: Photo **C** was taken at site 4.
  • Write down the direction in which the camera was pointing when each photo was taken.

4 The captions for photos **B** to **D** use words which may be new to you:
  residential   Central Business District   industrial
  • Write sentences to explain the meanings of these words.
  (☞ GLOSSARY)

In the Town

Residential zone

Industrial and residential zones

F is part of an O.S. map showing Galashiels. Galashiels is in a valley which has steep sides. We can tell this because the **contour lines** are close together. How do you think the valley has affected the shape of the town?

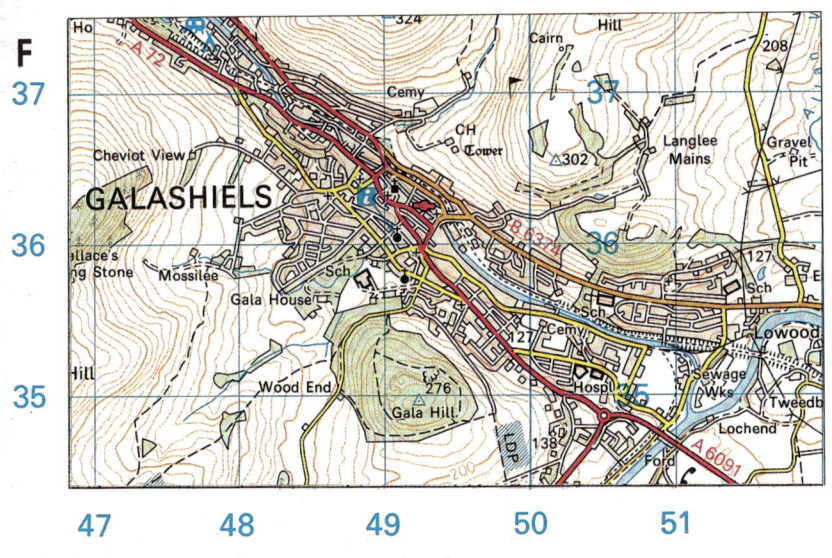

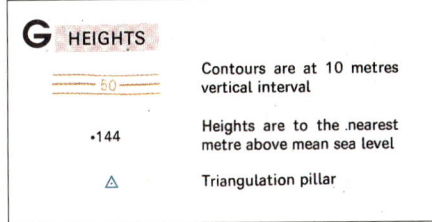

Height on O.S. maps

1:50 000 Ordnance Survey map extract

5 **E** shows different zones.
- Make a sketch of it and label three zones on it.

6 **G** shows three ways that height of the land can be shown on an O.S. map. These heights are in metres above sea-level.
- Find two contour lines with heights on the map **F**.
- For each one, write the height in metres and give its grid reference.
- Find these **spot heights** on the map:
   - 138
   - 127
   - 208
- For each, give its grid reference.
- Look at grid squares 5036 and 4934. Each contains a **triangulation pillar**.
- Write down their heights above sea-level.

EXTENSION ACTIVITY

7 For many years the main industry was wool milling.
- Find out why most wool milling towns in the UK have the following in common:
   - they are close to hill farms
   - they have a supply of soft water
   - they are close to fast flowing rivers

31

3.5 VAISON

Target

* To use what you have learned to look at a town abroad.
* To practice using map skills.

Vaison is a town in the Vaucluse area of the south of France. Every Tuesday there is a market in Vaison which brings people in from the surrounding countryside. People come to sell and buy things from the stalls in the streets. Towns which have markets are called **market towns**.

Vaison market

CORE ACTIVITIES

1 Look at **A** and at this list of words:
   summer winter street square empty
   busy sunny cloudy meat fruit
   ● Complete each of these sentences using one of the words in the list in each case:
   - This part of the market is in the _____.
   - The stall nearest the camera sells _____.
   - The weather is _____.
   - The season is _____.
   - The market is _____.

2 Photo **D** shows direction signs at a road junction.
   ● What is the name of the town past Malaucene?
   ● Which street are these signs on?
   ● Which mountain can you reach by turning left?
   ● Which way should you turn to go to the mini-golf?
   ● Draw the sign warning of the danger of falling rocks.

3 Look carefully at **C**.
   ● List five streets used by the Tuesday market.
   ● Which squares are each of the following found in:
     - Theatre Romain (Roman theatre)
     - Ecole Primaire (primary school)
     - Piscine (swimming pool)

4 Now look at **C** and **D** together.
   ● Where was the photographer standing when photo **D** was taken? Choose from the following grid squares:
     A1 C4 B4 A3 C1

5 Supposing that you were in a car driving west along the Quai Marechal Foch and you wanted to visit the Theatre Romain.
   ● Draw a sketch map to show how you would drive there.

In the Town

B	Galashiels	**Vaison**
Country		France
Population		5829
Main Street - name - number of specialist shops - number of catering services (hotels, cafes etc.)		Grand Rue 40 9
Land use zones		Central Business District. Houses on outskirts. Industry by river.

Two Towns Compared

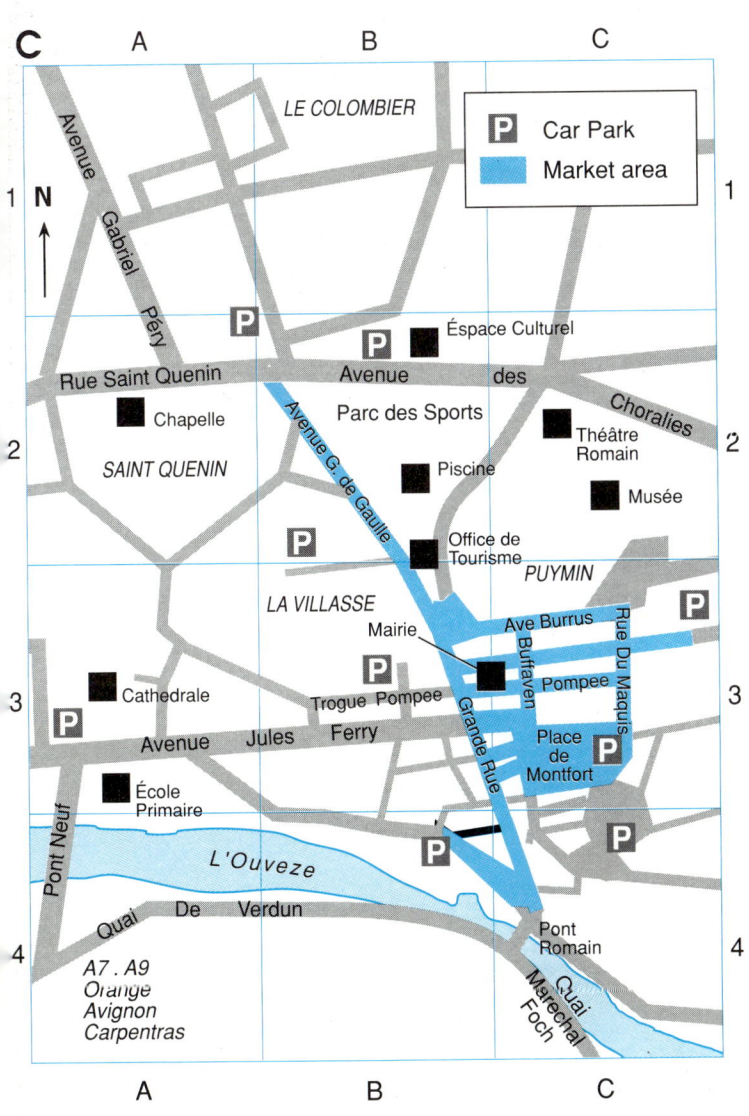

Street map of Vaison

Vaison has a population of 5 829 making it much smaller than Galashiels which has a population of 13 314. Do they have the same land-use pattern? **B** will help you decide. It gives some facts about Vaison but needs facts about Galashiels.

Road signs

EXTENSION ACTIVITY

6 On a copy of **B**:
- Fill in the empty boxes by using Units 3.1 to 3.4 to look up the facts you need.
- Write some sentences to describe ways that the two towns are alike and ways in which they are different.

33

4.1 BELFAST

Target

* To learn how cities grow from smaller settlements.
* To take information from a photograph.
* To read a **line graph**.
* To use an atlas to find place names.

In 1888 Queen Victoria gave Belfast a charter. This meant that Belfast could be called a city instead of a town. Two hundred years before that Belfast was no more than a village.

C shows how much the city grew in the nineteenth century. It grew so fast because a lot of new industries started up. People moved to the city for jobs.

In Belfast, the two main industries were shipbuilding and making linen cloth.

The city of Belfast

CORE ACTIVITIES

1 On photo **A** there are some letters marked. Each letter stands for one of these features:
   City Hall   River Lagan   office block
   shops   docks   blocks of flats
   open space   long straight street
   * Match each letter with the correct feature. EXAMPLE: A = blocks of flats.
   * Copy these statements about **A**.
     - The site is very hilly.
     - The city is densely built-up.
     - There is a lot of open space in the centre.
     - All the buildings are very tall.
     - The city centre has a lot of houses.
     - There is countryside in the distance.
   * Say which are true.

2 Find a map of Northern Ireland in your atlas.
   * Use it to name the places shown on **B**.
     (*HINT*: The letters shown are the first letters of each place name)

3 Northern Ireland has six counties. One is called County Down.
   * Make a list of all six names.
   * For each county, write down its main town.

4 **C** shows a **line graph** and a table. The line graph shows how many people were living in Belfast between 1840 and 1988.
   * Use the graph to complete the table. You will need to make a copy of the table first.

Cities grow

B

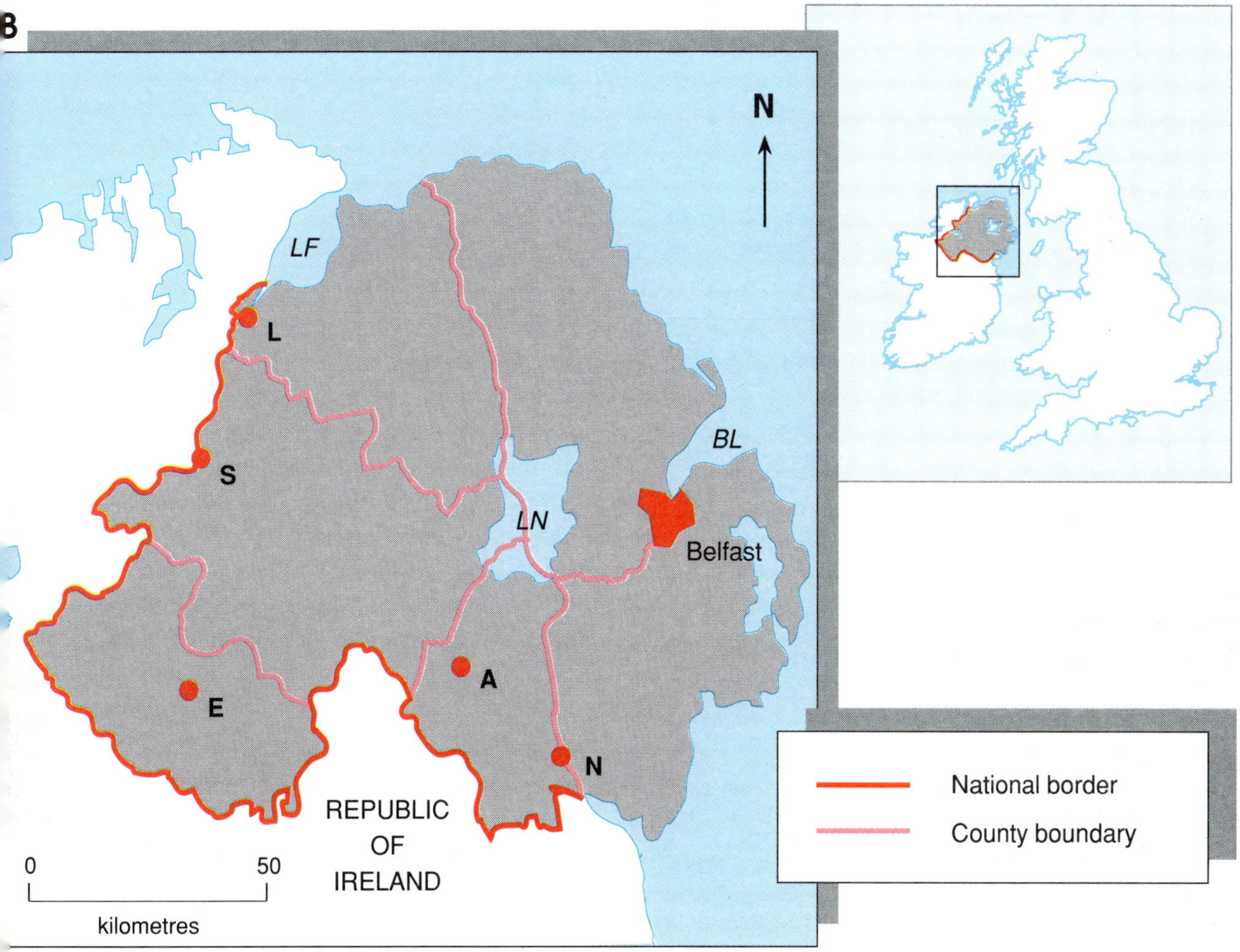

Northern Ireland

C

YEAR	1840	1860	1900				2000
POPULATION (thousands)	60	120	240				

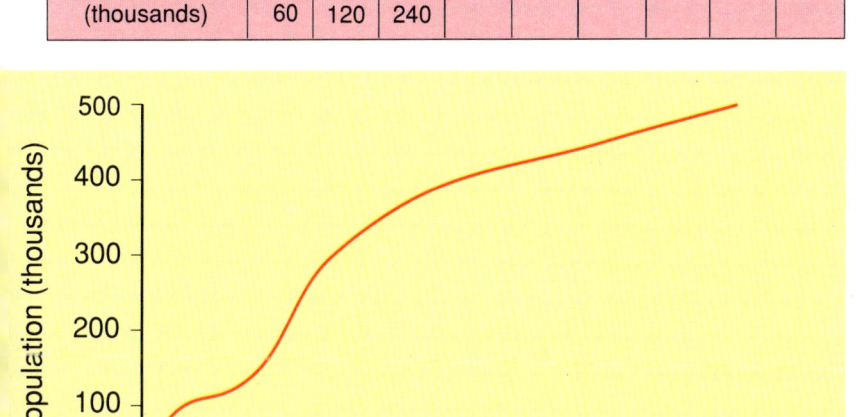

The population of Belfast

EXTENSION ACTIVITIES

5 Look at the list of features and statements in Activity 1.
  - For a town or city you know, write a short description of what it looks like.

6 Using your atlas:
  - Make a list of some names of rivers, mountains and places in Northern Ireland.
  - Use these to design a Northern Ireland word puzzle for someone else to do. It could be a wordsearch, a crossword, or a jumbled names list.

35

4.2 BIGGER AND BIGGER

Target

* To understand how cities grow.
* To realise that large cities can cause problems for people.
* To learn the locations of some main cities of the British Isles.

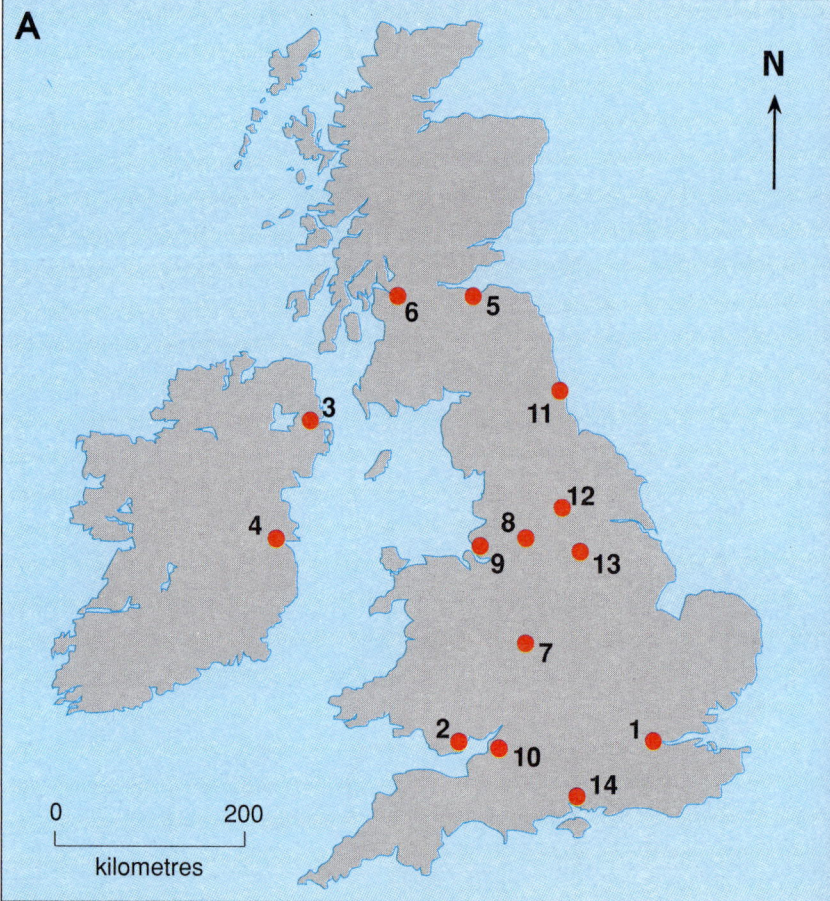

The location of large cities in the British Isles

As cities grow larger, they take up more space and there are more people living in them. **A** shows the location of large cities in the British Isles.

Belfast has grown from a small settlement at the mouth of the River Lagan into a city that now takes up 154 square kilometres of land. The growth of this city is shown by **B**.

CORE ACTIVITIES

1 Look carefully at the position of the cities shown by **A**.
 ● Use your atlas to name them.

2 Look at **B**, which gives information about the city of Belfast.
 ● Copy and complete these sentences about Belfast using words from the list at the end:
  - Belfast is at the mouth of the River _____ .
  - The city is at the _____ end of Belfast _____ .
  - Most of the city is _____ of the river.
  - Belfast has grown _____ .
  Lough   west   outwards   south   Lagan
 ● Use the scale to measure how far it is from the mouth of the river to the edge of the city in each of these directions:
  - North
  - South
  - East
  - West
  Give your answer to the nearest kilometre.
 ● Use the information about the city growth of Belfast to make a bar graph.

3 **C** shows some problems which are common to cities.
 ● Write sentences to say which pictures show each of these city problems:
  - traffic jams
  - **pollution**
  - using up farmland
  - the **decay** of old houses
  EXAMPLE: Picture 1 shows the problem of traffic jams in cities.

4 Read the following statements, which are about large cities:
  - People move away from the **inner city** areas.
  - They tend to grow outwards into the countryside.
  - Many people travel into cities for work.
  - As cities grow there are more cars and industry.
 ● Match each one of these statements to one of the problems listed in Activity 3.
  EXAMPLE: People moving away from inner city areas causes the decay of old houses.

36

Cities grow

B

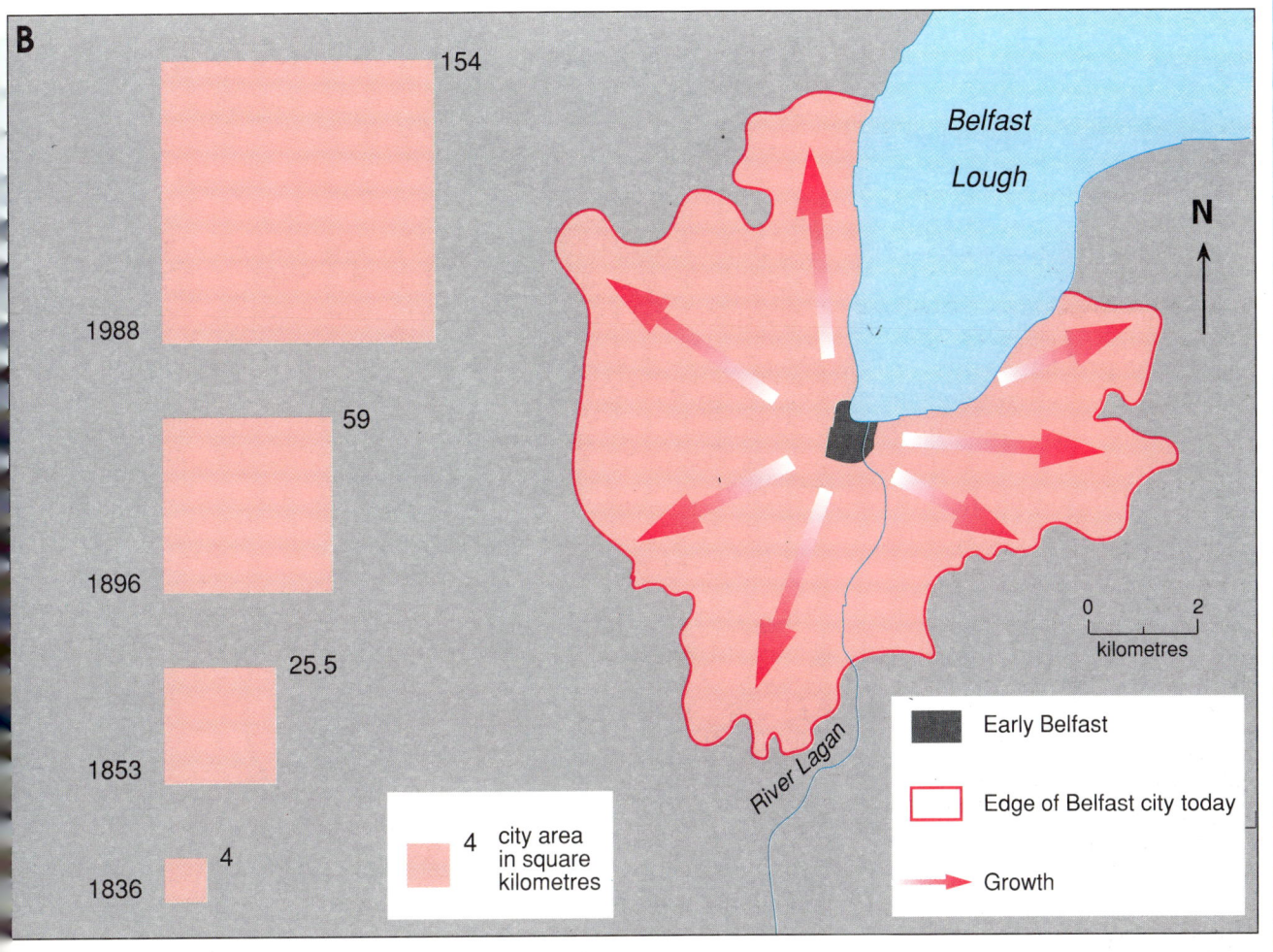

The growth of Belfast

City area in square kilometres:
- 1988: 154
- 1896: 59
- 1853: 25.5
- 1836: 4

Map legend:
- Early Belfast
- Edge of Belfast city today
- Growth

Problems of large cities

1. (traffic congestion)
2. (industrial pollution)
3. (graffiti - "SKINS RULE OK", "MILLWALL")
4. (Mullen Homes - Acquire another prime site for quality Executive Homes. Tel. 0040. 200)

EXTENSION ACTIVITIES

5 You have read a letter in the local paper saying that cars should be banned from the centre of your nearest city. This is to make it easier for the buses to get in and out of the centre. The letter also says that everybody should use buses rather than their own cars.
- Write a letter in reply. You may wish to agree or disagree with the idea.

6 Think about one of the problems that large cities have.
- Design a poster to show how and why it is a problem.

4.3 KEEPING CITIES IN

Target

* To learn what a **Green Belt** is.
* To understand how Green Belts limit the growth of cities.
* To introduce some differing views about Green Belts.

One of the problems with growing cities is that they use up farmland. As cities grow outwards, the countryside is built on. This means there is less land to grow food on, and less open country for people from **urban areas** to visit. The **environment** can be spoilt.

To stop this happening, many cities in the British Isles have **Green Belts**. A Green Belt is an area of land around cities which is to be kept as countryside. People are not normally allowed to build on Green Belt land. The idea is to stop cities growing outwards and not allow them to eat up the countryside as they grow.

In the case of Belfast, it was decided in 1964 not to allow the city to grow outwards any more. The edge of the city became the 'stopline'. Belfast would not be allowed to grow beyond it.

The Green Belt idea

CORE ACTIVITIES

1 **A** shows the Green Belt idea.
  * Use it to help you complete each of these sentences:
    - The city is growing _____.
    - The old village was _____.
    - The city is kept in by the _____ _____.
    - The country village is _____.
    - The smaller town _____ as new building jumps over the _____ _____.

2 Read this page carefully.
  * Now answer these questions in sentences in your own words:
    - What is a Green Belt?
    - What is the purpose of Green Belts?
    - What does Belfast have instead of a Green Belt?
    - Give two reasons why the countryside around cities should be protected.

Cities grow

Green Belts are a way of planning city growth so as to suit as many people as possible. However, some people feel that some building should be allowed. Not everyone agrees about how much building Green Belts should have. Sometimes buildings are allowed in the Green Belt. The frozen food factory in **B** is an example. When it was built it provided 400 jobs in an area where jobs were difficult to find. The company which built the factory liked the site because it is beside good dual carriageway roads.

A factory in a Green Belt

Views about Green Belts

Speech bubbles:
- IF THE CITY GROWS AND GROWS THERE'LL BE NOWHERE TO GO FOR CLEAN AIR OR PEACE AND QUIET.
- YOU CAN'T STOP PROGRESS WE DON'T WANT TO LIVE IN A GREEN MUSEUM
- Farmland should be KEPT To grow food for US ALL
- PEOPLE IN THE CITY NEED THE GREEN BELT
- THE COUNTRYSIDE SHOULD BE KEPT. IT'S LOVELY HERE.
- THERE'S PLENTY OF WASTE LAND IN CITIES. PEOPLE SHOULD PUT HOUSES THERE.
- PEOPLE NEED HOUSES. THEY HAVE TO BE BUILT SOMEWHERE.

3 Think about ways in which the countryside can be protected.
- Design a poster about protecting the countryside. It should show how cities can put the countryside in danger. A colourful or dramatic picture might be best. Perhaps the idea of the city eating up the countryside will help you decide what to draw.

4 Read the views about Green Belts in **C**. Some of these people seem to want to allow some building in the Green Belt.
- Write down their views.
- Make a list of the views in **C** which seem to be in favour of leaving the Green Belt as countryside.

5 Here is a list of people who might have views about the factory in **B**:
- an unemployed local person
- a nature lover
- the factory manager
- Imagine talking to each of them. What would you expect each of them to say about whether the factory should have been built?

EXTENSION ACTIVITIES

6 As a person living in a small country village you are angry to discover a plan to build a new housing estate close to your house. You moved to the village only last year to escape from the city. The village is in the Green Belt. A television reporter is coming to interview you. She has given you a list of questions she wants to ask you. These are her questions:
  - What do you think of the housing estate idea?
  - Why should the Green Belt be protected?
  - Where are people to live if the houses are not built?
  - Are you not being selfish?
  - Why should more people from the city not live in the country like you do?
  - What will you do to try to stop the housing estate being built?
- Write down what you would say in reply to each question.

7 You decide to organise a petition to send to your M.P. This is a letter you want other people in the village to sign. Your M.P.'s name is Sarah Holmes.
- Write the letter you will send.
- Make very clear what your objections are.

4.4 CRAIGAVON

Target

* To understand that **New Towns** are planned.
* To discover the location of New Towns in the UK.
* To try to understand people's views about New Towns.

New towns are places which have been planned to take the pressure off the large cities. In the past, people have been encouraged to move into New Towns. There are over 30 New Towns in the United Kingdom. **A** shows where they are.

Craigavon is a New Town built close to Belfast. It is a place for people to live instead of them adding to the growing **population** of Belfast. Craigavon is going to be bigger than many New Towns when it is finished. It can really be called a New City.

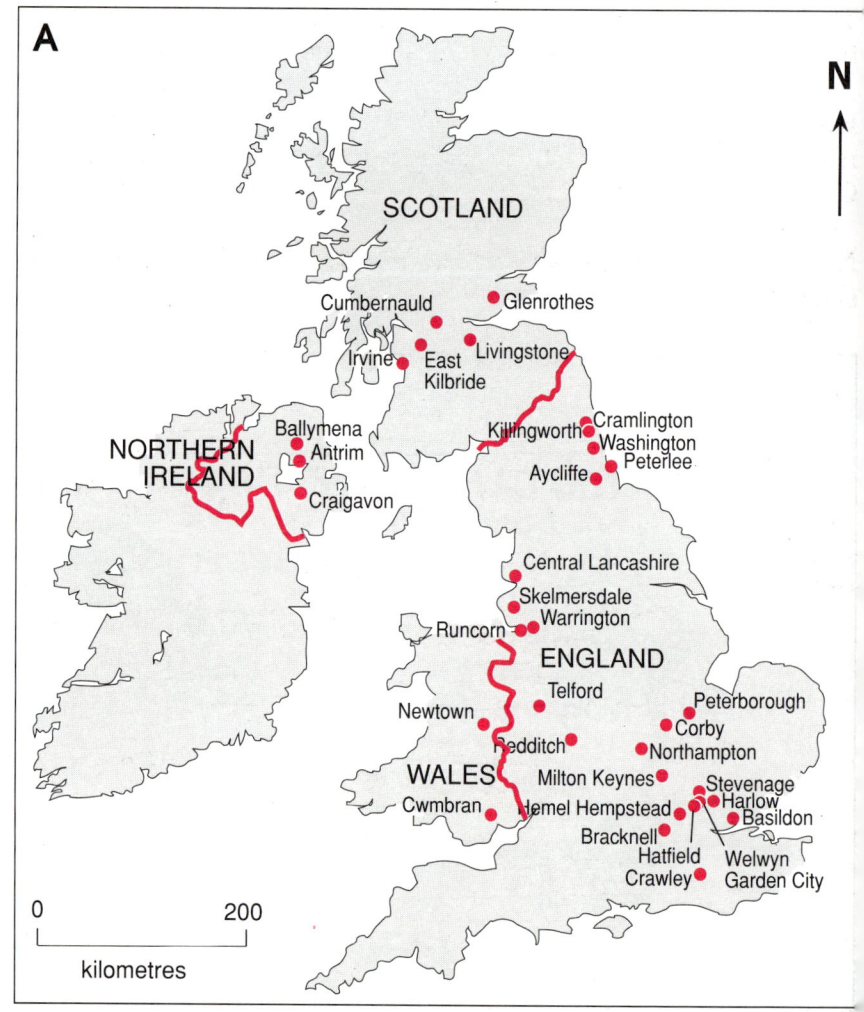

A

The location of New Towns in the UK

CORE ACTIVITIES

1 Look at **A**.
  * Copy and complete the following table by counting the number of New Towns in each country of the United Kingdom:

COUNTRY	NUMBER OF NEW TOWNS
England	
Northern Ireland	
Scotland	
Wales	

  * Make a bar graph, from the information in your completed table.
  * Which country has the most New Towns?
  * Make your own table to show the nearest large city to each of the new towns. Use an atlas to help you. Your table will need two columns.

2 The table below shows population figures for Craigavon.

YEAR	POPULATION
1965	40 000
1981	71 000
1985	100 000

  * Use these figures to draw a line graph. (*HINT*: Look back at the graph in Unit 4.1.)

3 **B** is a plan of Craigavon. Use it to answer these questions in sentences:
  * Which two old towns does Craigavon join together?
  * How many housing areas are shown?
  * List five things from the plan which are to do with **leisure** in Craigavon.
  * Approximately how long is the city of Craigavon?
  * What is found in the city centre?
  * Which motorway links Craigavon to Belfast?

Cities grow

The New City of Craigavon has been carefully planned. Places to live are kept separate from places to work, as **B** shows. Places for leisure have been included in the plan.

Housing areas in Craigavon have been planned in small **neighbourhood** estates. The idea of these neighbourhoods is to help people get to know each other and help each other to live happily in Craigavon. This idea has been tried in other New Towns too.

Not everyone is happy about New Towns though. A different view about life in a New Town is shown by **C**.

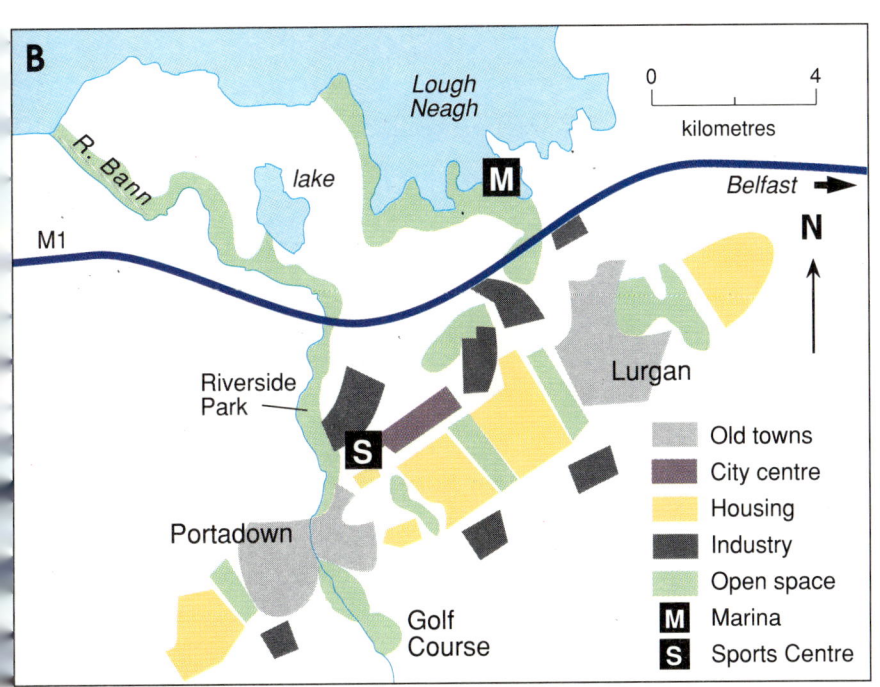

Plan of Craigavon

Nancy doesn't like it!

4 Here are some facts about the way Craigavon has been planned.
- Houses are in neighbourhoods.
- Industry and houses are kept separate.
- The sports centre is in the centre.
- Industry is close to the motorway.

Each of these things was done for one of the following reasons:
- to make it easy to get to
- to transport goods easily
- to keep down noise and pollution
- to help people live happily together

- Match up the facts and reasons to make four sentences.
  EXAMPLE: The sports centre is in the centre to make it easy to get to.

5 Look at **C**. Nancy lives with her parents in a New Town.
- From what you can see, describe the area where Nancy lives.
- Where do you think Nancy would like to live? Why?
- Her parents do like it. Use facts from this page to imagine what you would say to her if you were one of her parents. Talk about the houses and why it can be healthier to live outside cities.

EXTENSION ACTIVITY

6 New Towns like Craigavon want people to come and live in them. They want companies to open factories there.
- Think out a list of attractions Craigavon can offer.
- Use your list to design an advertisement to persuade people to come to Craigavon. It needs to tell them how good it is.
  Your advertisement can be for companies or ordinary people, but you need to be clear about which.

4.5 COPENHAGEN

Target

* To compare the growth of cities abroad with the growth of British cities.
* To see how Copenhagen has planned its **urban growth**.
* To learn the names of the countries and **capital** cities of the **European Community (EC)**.

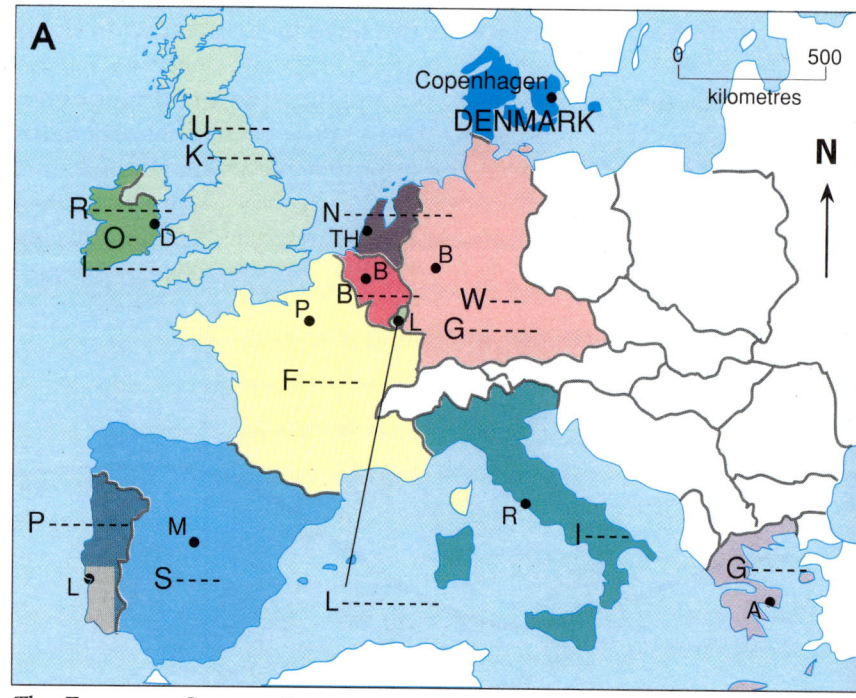

A

The European Community

Copenhagen is the capital city of Denmark. Denmark, like the United Kingdom, the Republic of Ireland and France, is a country belonging to the **EC**. **A** shows the twelve countries which belong to the EC and their **capital** cities. These are shown by colour on the map.

B

Copenhagen

CORE ACTIVITIES

1 Find a map of Europe in your atlas.
   - Use it to complete the names of the twelve EC countries shown on **A**.
   - Find out the names of the capital cities of each of the twelve countries.

2 **C** shows the region around Copenhagen.
   - Use the map to complete these sentences, using place names:
     - Copenhagen is on the coast of a narrow sea called ___ ___ .
     - Across the sea is another country called ___ .
     - Copenhagen airport is on the island of ___ .
     - Two other Danish islands on the map are ___ and ___ .
     - Five towns around Copenhagen are ___ , ___ , ___ , ___ and ___ .

3 **C** also shows the motorways around Copenhagen.
   - Match each of these Danish motorways with the direction in which they leave the city. The directions here are next to the wrong motorway.
     - E66   north west
     - 21   north
     - 16   south west
     - E4   west

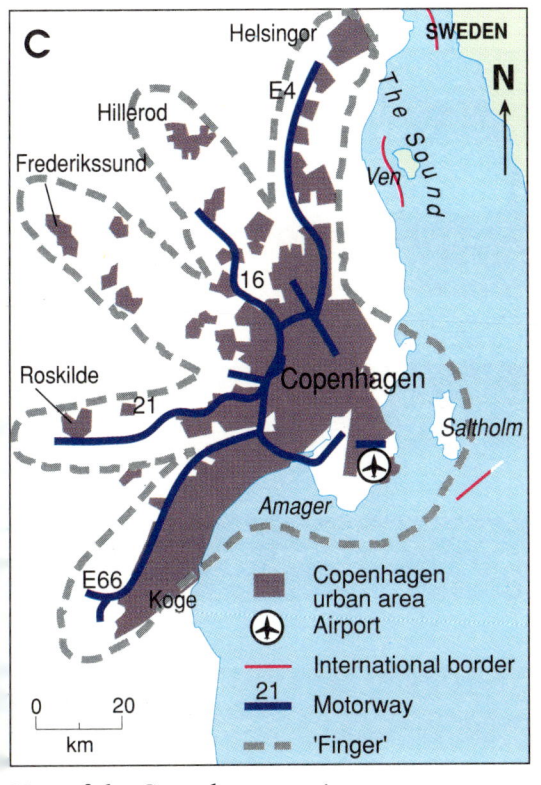

Cities grow

C

Map of the Copenhagen region

Like Belfast, and other British Isles cities, Copenhagen grew outwards as its population went up.

However, the **urban growth** of Copenhagen was planned differently. Instead of a stopline or a Green Belt to keep the city in, Copenhagen was allowed to keep growing. To save countryside, building was only allowed close to the five main routes in and out of the city.

In Denmark these strips of building are called 'fingers'. Between the fingers are areas of open space for farms and for leisure. The whole plan is called the 'Finger Plan'.

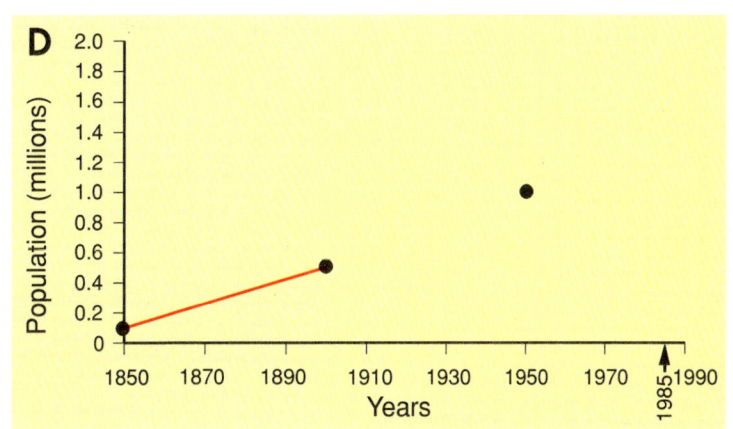

D

Year	Population (millions)
1850	0.1
1900	0.5
1950	1.0
1960	1.5
1970	1.8
1985	1.4

The growth of Copenhagen

4 You will need an atlas and an outline map of Denmark. On an outline map of Denmark, mark and label these features:
- Seas: North Sea
  Skagerrak Kattegat
  The Sound (Oresund)
- Land areas: Jutland (Jylland) Funen (Fyn) Zeeland (Sjaelland)
- Nearby countries: Sweden West Germany
- Towns and cities: Copenhagen Odense Aarhus Aalborg Esbjerg
  The names in brackets are in Danish. Your atlas may use these.

5 **D** shows population figures for Copenhagen.
- Use these to finish the line graph that has been started.
- Copy and complete this writing about your line graph:
  In 1850 the number of people in Copenhagen was only _____ . The population reached a million in ____ and hit its peak of nearly _ million in ____ . Since then it has gone down again.

6 Using the information on these pages, answer the following questions:
- How is Copenhagen's growth like Belfast's?
- How has Copenhagen's growth been planned differently?
- Where is building allowed in Copenhagen?
- What is between the 'fingers'?

EXTENSION ACTIVITY

7 You will need an atlas and an outline map of **A**.
- Make a list of all the other countries shown on **A**.
- Mark them and their capital cities on an outline map of Europe. You may need a key.

43

5.1 URBAN DECAY

Target

* To understand about **urban decay**.
* To consider the views of people affected by urban decay.

An **urban** area is a built-up area. Towns and cities are urban areas. In some parts of urban areas, buildings have decayed. These may even be pulled down leaving empty spaces and waste land. This has often happened in inner cities, as **A** shows.

Inner cities are the older parts of cities close to the city centre. Britain's main cities (**B**) have been affected by **urban decay**.

Urban decay

CORE ACTIVITIES

1 Look carefully at photo **A**.
   * From this list of words choose five which you think describe the scene of urban decay:
     wasteland   bustling   old   rich   attractive   modern   empty   sad   cheerful   ugly

2 (☞ GLOSSARY)
   * Write sentences to explain the meanings of each of these:
     - urban
     - inner city
     - **rural**

3 Read **C**. The people here are talking about the past but they each remember it differently.
   * Make two lists, one of the good things they remember and one of the bad things remembered.

4 Imagine yourself as one of the old people in **C** when they were your age.
   * Write a few sentences to describe what life would have been like. **C** will help give you ideas.

5 Find a map in your atlas showing cities in the British Isles.
   * Use it to complete the names of the cities shown on a copy of **B**.
   * Make a table to show these cities. Next to each one write down the country it belongs to.
   * Add these labels to your map:
     England   Scotland   Wales   Northern Ireland
     Eire   English Channel   North Sea   Irish Sea
     Atlantic Ocean

Putting Places Right

B

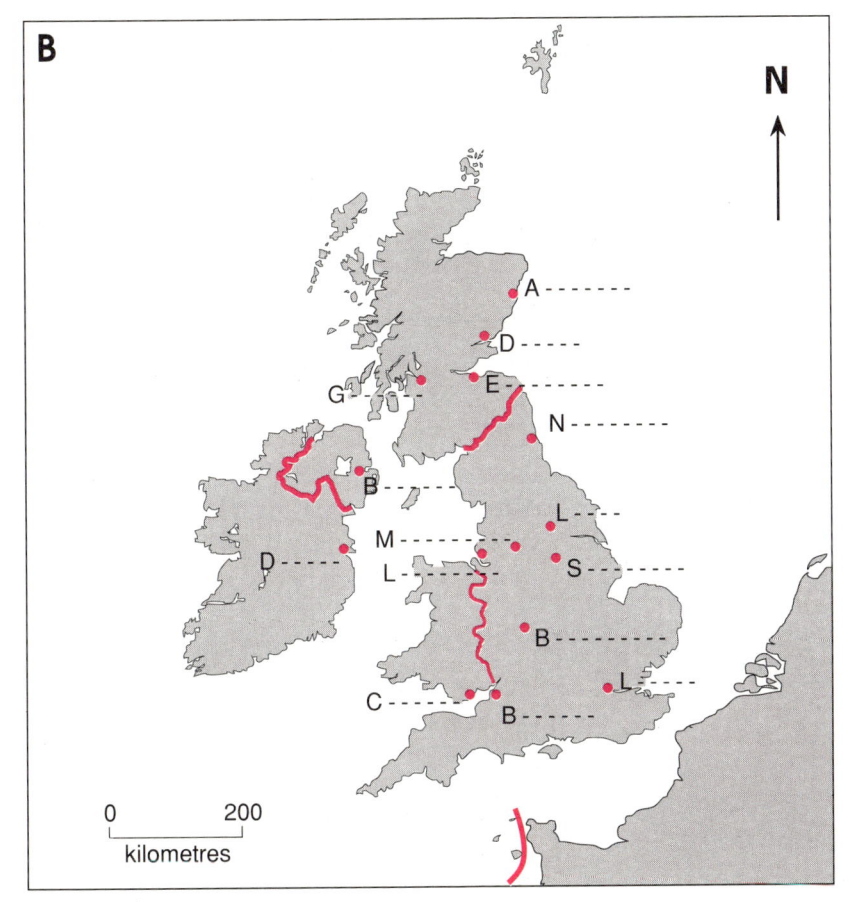

Britain's largest cities

C

"THERE USED TO BE PLENTY OF JOBS IN THE DOCKS AND THE FACTORIES. THEY'VE ALL GONE NOW."

"IT USED TO BE REALLY LIVELY HERE. THERE WERE ALWAYS CHILDREN PLAYING IN THE STREETS."

"PEOPLE TALK ABOUT THE GOOD OLD DAYS. THERE WEREN'T ANY. I WAS UNEMPLOYED WHEN I WAS YOUNG. WHEN I DID HAVE A JOB IT WAS BADLY PAID."

"EVERYBODY KNEW EVERYBODY ELSE. WE ALL HELPED EACH OTHER."

"HOUSES HERE WERE NEVER MUCH. FOR YEARS WE HAD NO BATHROOM."

"THERE'S CRIME EVERYWHERE NOW. YOU USED TO BE ABLE TO LEAVE YOUR DOOR OPEN ALL DAY."

When I was young...

EXTENSION ACTIVITIES

6 Think about an urban place you know.
 • Are there any areas of urban decay?
 • Draw a sketch to show what it is like.
 • Put some labels on your sketch to help explain what it shows.

7 Talk to an old person about what life was like when they were your age. You could start by asking them if they agree with any of the views in **C**.
 • Use what they say to write a report.

45

5.2 CARDIFF DOCKS

A

KILOMETRES

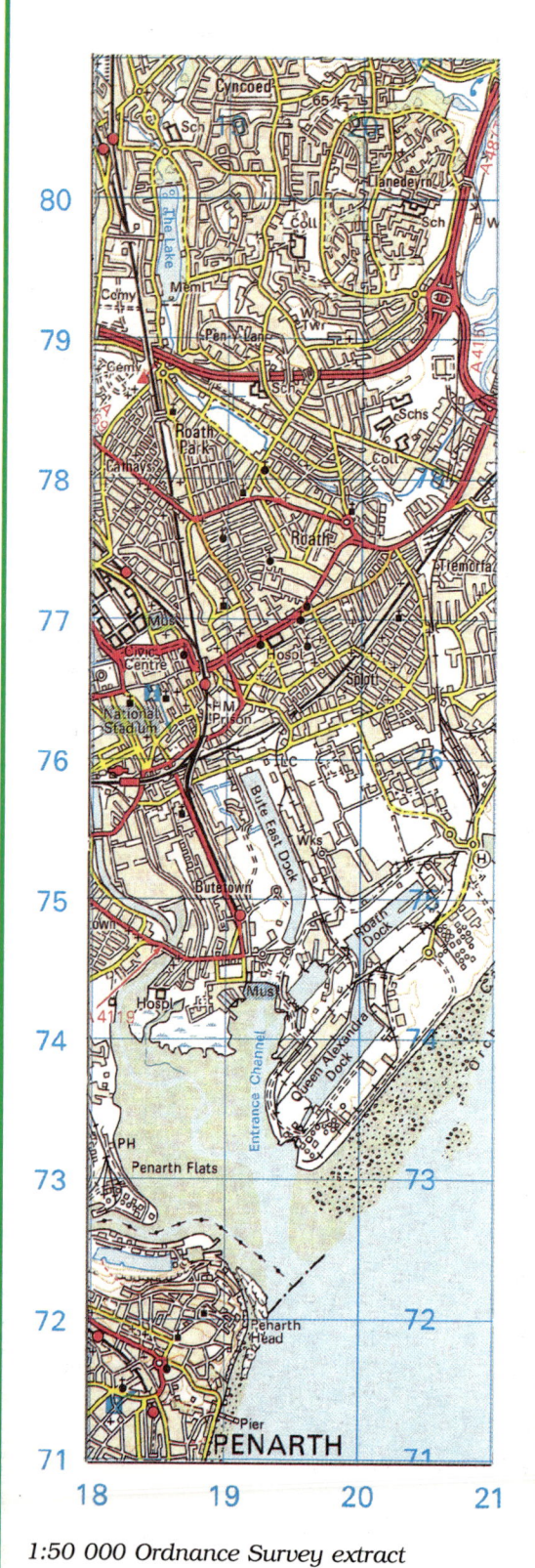

Target

* To understand that trade can be linked to urban decay in dockland areas.
* To draw a map to show the location of Cardiff.
* To use a line graph.
* To measure distance on an O.S. map extract.

A hundred years ago Cardiff was the busiest port in the British Isles (**B**). Today the picture is very different as **C** shows. For most of the time in between the weight of cargo handled by Cardiff Docks fell as you can see from the line graph in **D**. Less trade meant less work, less money and more decay.

A is part of an O.S. map. It shows Cardiff docks and the city's Central Business District. The map has been drawn at a scale of 1:50 000. This means that every 2 centimetres on the map represents 1 kilometre on the ground.

B

The docks in the past

1:50 000 Ordnance Survey extract

CORE ACTIVITIES

1 Look at **B** and **C** together.
* Copy and complete this writing about them, using the words below:
The black and white photograph shows the docks of the ____ . The docks of ____ are shown by the ____ photograph. In the past the docks were ____ and most of the ships were ____ ships. Today there are still ships but not very ____ .
many   today   sailing   busy   air   past

Putting Places Right

2 Using the map extract and its scale:
- Measure and write down the real lengths of these docks:
  - Bute East
  - Roath
  - Queen Alexandra
- How far are these docks from the CBD?
  (*HINT*: Measure the length of the straight road going north west from Butetown)

3 **C** is an **aerial photograph**.
- Make an outline sketch of **C**.
- Add these labels:
  flat land   dock   warehouse
  yachts   city   marshy area

4 Study **D** very carefully before choosing the right answer to each of these:
- The graph shows the years from:
  1920   1960   1820
- The graph shows years up to:
  1960   1990   1820
- The most cargo was about:
  2 million tons   14 million tons   24 million tons
- The most cargo was in:
  1960   1931   1913
- In 1960 the weight of cargo was:
  2 million tons   14 million tons   20 million tons
  EXAMPLE: The graph shows the years from 1820.

5 Answer each of these questions in sentences:
- What happened to the weight of cargo between 1820 and 1913?
- What was happening to the weight of cargo between 1920 and 1960?
- Give the name of this type of graph.

6 **E** shows the location of Cardiff and ten other places in Wales.
- Use an atlas to name these places.

Cardiff docks today

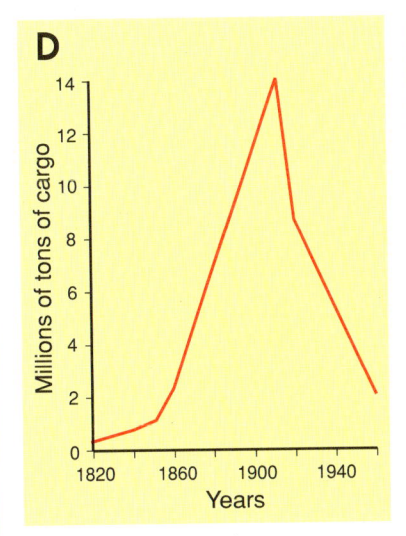

Cardiff's dock trade

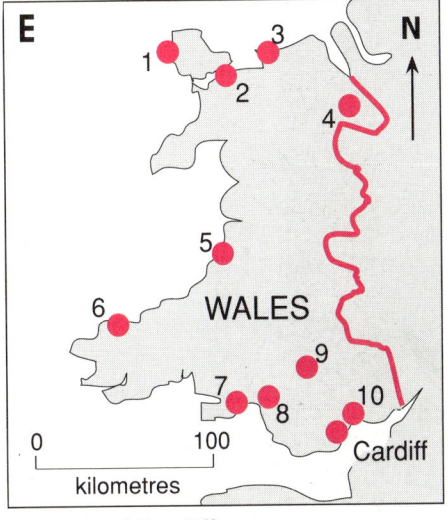

Location of Cardiff

EXTENSION ACTIVITIES

7 Look again at **D.**
- Make a table of statistics showing the weight of cargo every 20 years from 1850 onwards.

8 You will need an atlas showing a map of Wales.
- Unjumble the place names in the following sentences:
  - The main mountains in Wales are the RMINCBAA Mountains. The largest island in Wales is called GSAEYLEN.
  - This island is separated from the mainland by the NAMIE Straits.
  - West of Swansea Bay is RAAHETCMNR Bay.
  - North of Cardigan Bay is FNRCENAROA Bay.
  - The river in Aberystwyth is the HWTTYS.

5.3 WHAT'S BEING DONE?

Target

* To learn how areas of urban decay can be put right or renewed.
* To see how **urban renewal** can improve the environment's looks and safety.

The dockland area of Cardiff is being changed and parts of it rebuilt. This is called **urban renewal.**
Urban renewal like this has taken place in many cities. For example, in Bristol, Liverpool, London and Newcastle-upon-Tyne.

In the Cardiff Bay area, new homes, offices, shops, industry and waterside leisure services are being created.
The aim is to make Cardiff Bay one of the most attractive living and working environments in the world.

An example of urban renewal

CORE ACTIVITIES

1 Look at **A** carefully.
   - What is the name of the street?
   - What is the corporation called?

2 **A** has numbers on it from 1 to 5.
   - Match each number to one of the environmental improvements listed here:
     new pavements   new lamp-post   trees
     bollards   kerb sticking out
   - What are your feelings about the street? Write down things you like or dislike about it.

3 Using **B**:
   - Copy and complete this description of the Spiller's Building. Use the words at the end.
     The old Spiller's Building is an unusual shape, a _____ . It is made of _____ with a wooden _____ house on top. It is in bad condition. _____ are growing out of it. All around the building is _____ . It stands next to a _____ .
     wasteland   lift   weeds   canal   triangle   brick
   - Make a sketch of **B** and add labels.

Putting Places Right

B and **D** show a big warehouse before and after renewal. This warehouse was built in 1896 and is called the Spiller's Building. It is being made into 47 flats by a company called Lovell Urban Renewal. It is going to make the middle open with a glass roof, and the flats will have balconies.

The Spiller's Building

An artist's impression

EXTENSION ACTIVITIES

4 **D** is an artist's impression. It shows what the side of the building facing the canal will finally look like.
- How can you tell it shows that side? Write a sentence to explain.
- Write a short description of **D** to say what improvements it shows.
- Draw what you think the end of the building facing the road will look like when it is finished.

5 Think of a street or building you know which has been renewed.
- Prepare a report on it. This could include drawings as well as writing and should show people what changes have been made, and why.
- Say what you like or dislike about what has been done.

6 The Spiller's building is being renewed by a company called Lovell Urban Renewal which is working with the Cardiff Bay Development Corporation. When it is finished it will have to sell the 47 flats.
- Design an attractive advertisement it could put in a newspaper to try to persuade people to come and look at the new flats. Use this page for ideas.

5.4 THE ISSUES RAISED

Target

* To recognise and consider some issues raised by urban renewal.

People often have different views about urban renewal and sometimes renewal schemes can create issues.

Two common issues are jobs and housing. Local people may, for example, be concerned that new housing will be too expensive for them or that old established communities will be destroyed. They may also be worried that there will be few jobs for them or that the shops and services planned will be designed for tourists rather than them.

One of the main parts of the Cardiff Bay scheme is the building of a **barrage** to shut Cardiff Bay off from the sea. This is being done to create waterside leisure areas. People have very different views about the effects of this too.

A

- SOME OF THE NEW HOUSES ARE TOO EXPENSIVE FOR US.
- THE NEW MARINA WILL COST TOO MUCH FOR US TO KEEP OUR BOATS THERE.
- OUR STREET'S GOING TO BE IMPROVED. HOW? NO-ONE HAS TOLD US.
- THE BIRDS WHO LIVE IN THE BAY COULD DIE WHEN THE LAKE IS MADE.
- THE NEW LAKE IS TO BE USED FOR LEISURE, BUT THE WATER IS BADLY POLLUTED.

Different views. What are your views about urban renewal?

CORE ACTIVITIES

1 A recent newspaper story about the Cardiff Bay scheme included the views shown in **A**.
- Read these views and think carefully about them.
- Decide what you might do to reassure these people and convince them that the scheme is a good thing for Cardiff.
- Write down what you would do and explain why.

2 Read page 51.
- List five things which Cardiff Bay Development Corporation says about the Cardiff Bay scheme.
- How important do you think these changes are for people living in the area?
- Imagine you are a local resident. Try to list these five changes in their order of importance. Start with the most important first.
- How important are they for the city of Cardiff?

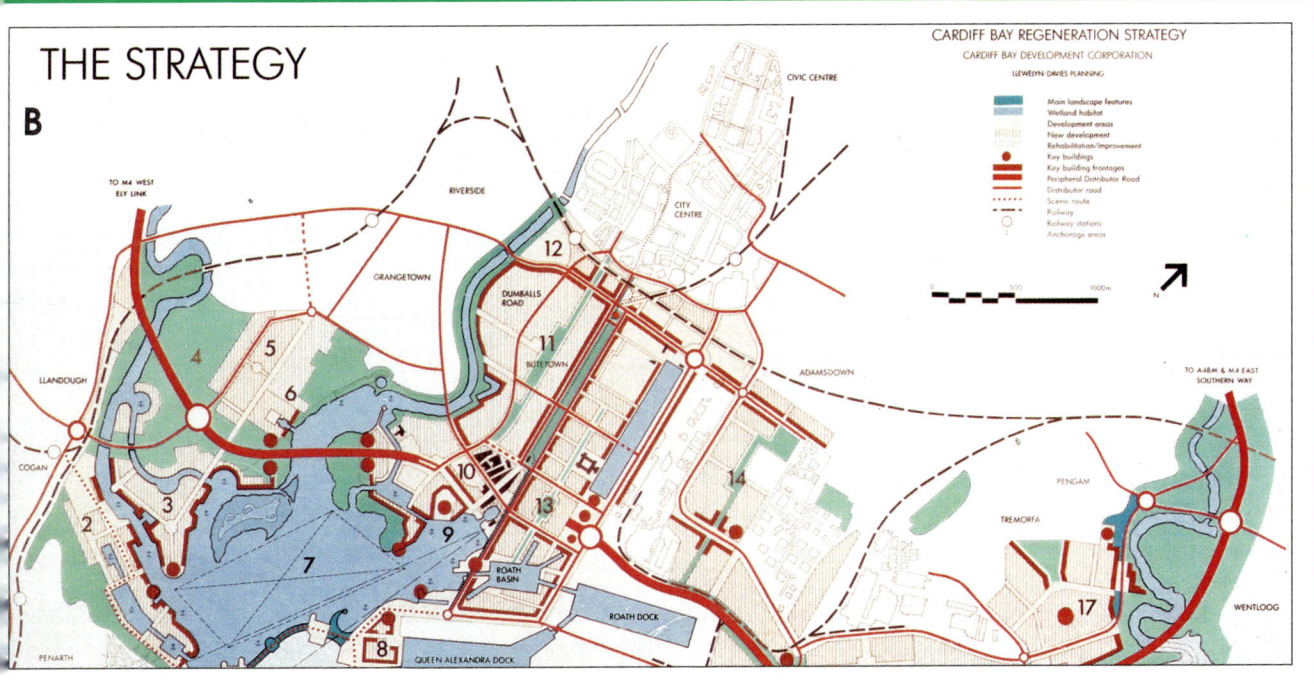

Putting Places Right

THE STRATEGY

Map of the proposed scheme

Cardiff Bay Development Corporation is in charge of the scheme to renew the dockland area of the city. It says it will create lots of new homes along a 16 kilometre waterfront and that it will be an exciting place to live. Areas of decay will be put right. New jobs will come and there will be new leisure facilities like a marina for sailing boats.

The Cardiff Bay barrage

3 Look at **B**. It shows the Development Areas.
- What direction would you be travelling in if you went in a straight line, between the following pairs of places?
  - Adamsdown to Roath Dock
  - Ely fields to Alexandra Head
  - Butetown to Area 12
  - Penarth to Queen Alexandra Dock
  EXAMPLE: Adamsdown to Roath Dock is south.
- Use the scale on **B** to measure the straight line distances between each of these pairs of places.

4 **C** is an artist's impression of how the barrage might look.
- Which two areas of water will it separate?
- What is a **fresh water lake**?
  (☞ GLOSSARY)
- Write down three leisure uses that could be made of the fresh water lake.

EXTENSION ACTIVITY

5 Think carefully about what you have read and looked at on these pages.
- You are a reporter, writing for a national newspaper, and have been asked to write an article about the Cardiff Bay renewal scheme.
- Write your article, remembering to show all points of view.
  The article will be read by people who have never heard of the scheme before.

5.5 DIEPPE

Target

* To compare a foreign urban improvement scheme with the one in Cardiff Bay.
* To use an atlas to find places' names.

Dieppe is a port on the coast of Normandy in northern France. Many buildings in the old town were built nearly 300 years ago. In 1694 Dieppe was nearly destroyed by fire. When it was rebuilt much care was taken over the look of the new buildings but as the years went by they were allowed to decay until they reached the state shown in **A**.

Residence Sainte-Catherine 1981

B shows a block of building in Dieppe called the Residence Sainte-Catherine. This building has been modernised to make 51 homes which are rented cheaply to local Dieppe people. The work was done mainly by a housing group called Sodineuf.

Residence Sainte-Catherine now

CORE ACTIVITIES

1 Look carefully at the building in **B**.
   - Is it finished?
   - How many homes does it provide?
   - Who are the homes for?
   - Who did the work?

2 **C** is the start of a table to show some features that modernised places often have.
   - Look at **A**.
   - Which of the features shown in **C** can you see in photo **B**?
   - For each one you find put a tick in the Sainte-Catherine column. The first one has been done.

3 Look back to **A** and **C** in Unit 5.3.
   - Put ticks in the Angelina Street and Spiller's Building column to show the features you can see.

4 On an outline sketch of **B**:
   - label each of the renewal features it has.

5 Use your table to decide on three features of urban renewal which seem to be most common.
   - Write them down.

Putting Places Right

6 Read about the Spiller's Building again, using Unit 5.3. Look at **C** in Unit 5.4. as well.
- Write new answers to the questions in Activity 1. This time your answer will be about the Spiller's Building.
- Say which of these statements you agree with, and which you disagree with. Explain why.
  - French and British urban renewal schemes look the same.
  - They house different sorts of people.
  - Two places are enough to decide if French and British urban renewal is the same.

7 Map **D** shows the location of Dieppe.
- Use a key to name the towns and cities shown by the numbers 1 to 10 on **D**. These are the names you are looking for:
  Paris   Lyon   Marseille
  Le Havre   Bordeaux
  Toulouse   Strasbourg   Lille
  Nantes   St. Etienne
- Add these sea labels to a copy of **D**:
  English Channel   Bay of Biscay   Mediterranean Sea   Strait of Dover

8 Using an atlas:
- Unjumble the place names near the ends of these sentences:
  - France's highest mountains are the SLAP.
  - The mountains along the Spanish border are called RENSEPNEY.
  - The river at Paris is the EESIN.
  - Two big rivers in western France are the LIREO and the NODIGER.
  EXAMPLE: France's highest mountains are the Alps.

C

FEATURE	Sainte-Catherine	Angelina Street	Spiller's Building
cleaned bricks	✓		
new roof			✓
replacement windows			
white paintwork			
traditional lamp			
new paving			
trees			
bollards			

Features of urban renewal

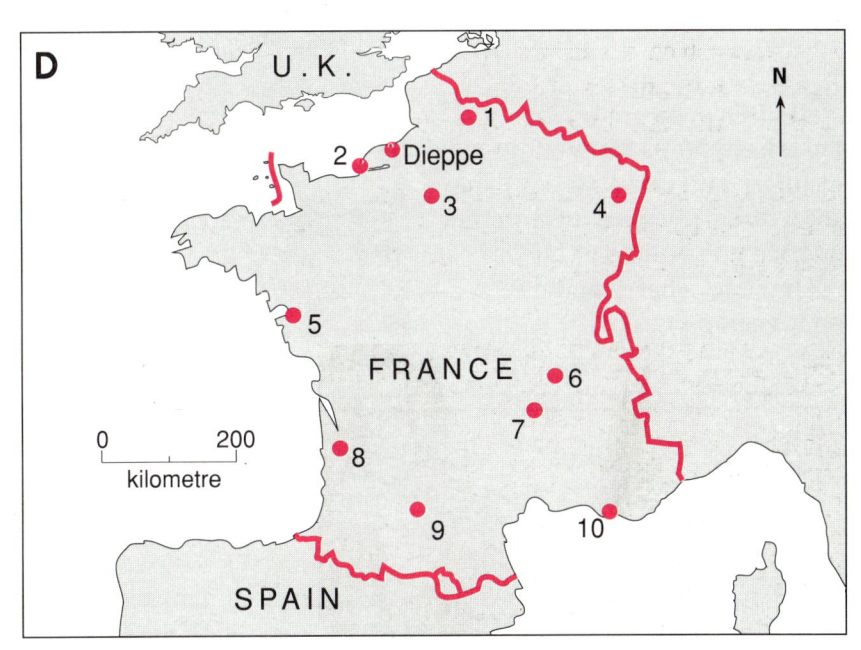

D

Location of Dieppe

EXTENSION ACTIVITIES

9 Using **A**:
- Make a sketch of one of the buildings shown.
- Add labels to your sketch. The labels should point out the building's decay.

10 Use a table like the one in **C** to survey some buildings that you know of, in the area where you live, that have been modernised.
- Make labelled sketches of the buildings you survey.
- Write some sentences to describe ways in which they are similar to the buildings in Units 5.3 and 5.5 and the ways in which they are different.

6.1 NEIL'S PHOTO SHOP

Target

* To realise that the places people use to make a living are part of geography.
* To understand that a shop may offer a variety of **goods** and services.
* To use a road map to give directions.

Neil Fletcher is a photographer. He runs his business from a shop in Tynemouth (**A**). The address is 8 Percy Park Road.

Neil often goes out on jobs. He takes photos for weddings, industry and newspapers. The shop offers a variety of different **goods** and services to Neil's customers. These can be seen on the shop plan (**B**).

Neil's shop

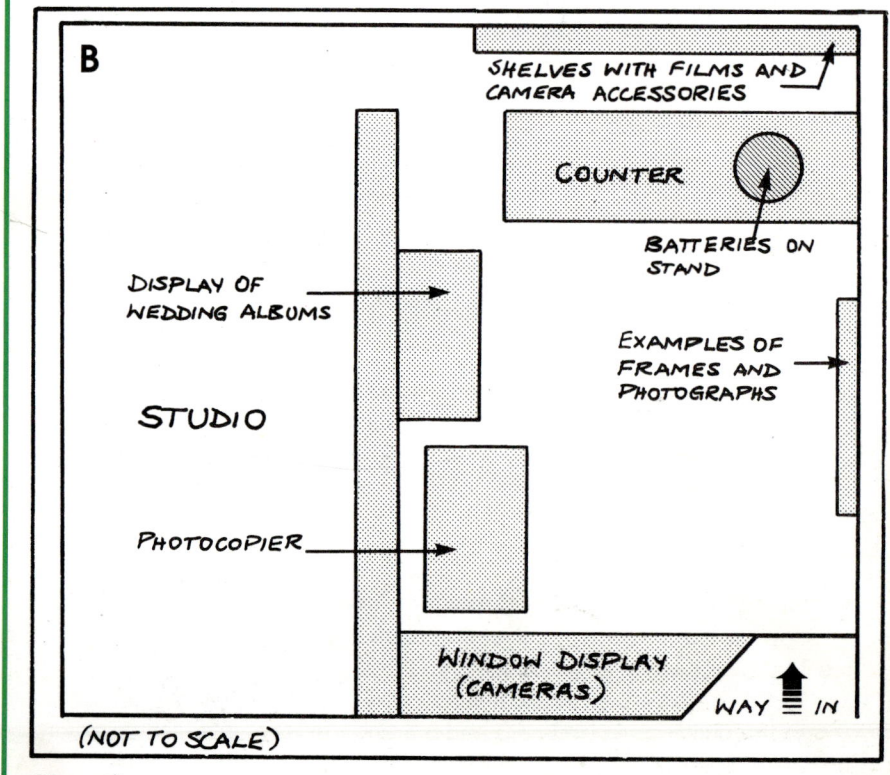

Shop plan

CORE ACTIVITIES

1 Look at **A** and **B** together.
  - Where is Neil standing?
  - On a copy of the plan (**B**) mark where both Neil and the photographer were standing.
  - Shade in the part of the shop that the photo shows.

2 Look at **B**.
  - Write a list of seven things that Neil sells or the services he offers for his customers.

Making a Living

C

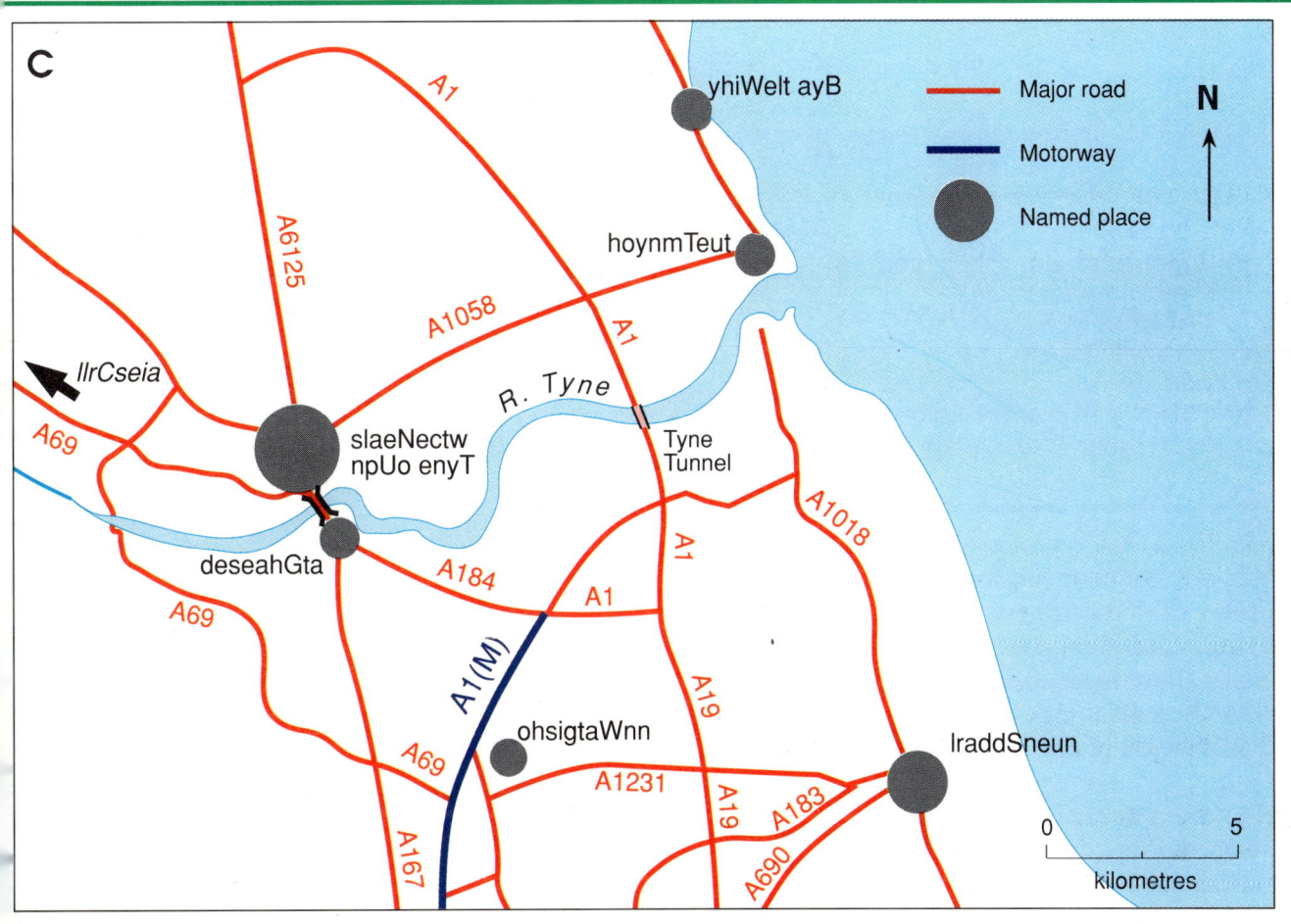

Road map

The road map (**C**) shows the places that are connected with Neil's business. Most of the weddings he photographs are in Whitley Bay, Cullercoats and Tynemouth. Sometimes he goes to Newcastle-upon-Tyne, Sunderland or even as far as Carlisle. Washington is where the customers' films go to be developed and the people who look after the photocopy machine come from Gateshead.

3 (☞ GLOSSARY)
- Find out what goods and services are.
- Write a sentence to explain the difference.
- Go back to the list you made for Activity 2.
- Decide which words are goods and which are services.
- Draw a ring around each of the goods.

4 Use **C** to help you complete this route description:
To get to the shop from Washington you start on the A 1231 road. Then you turn onto the A _____ . This leads onto the A _____ through the Tyne Tunnel. After that you turn right onto the A _____ which goes to Tynemouth.

5 Neil has just had a telephone call to say that somebody new is coming from Gateshead to service his photocopier.
- Write out the directions that Neil should give them.

EXTENSION ACTIVITIES

6 Shops are often carefully planned. Think about the way Neil's shop is planned.
- Why do you think that the goods are behind the counter?
- Why is the studio separate?
- Why is the photocopier on its own in the corner?
- Label a copy of the shop plan to give reasons for these three things and for others you think of.

7 Find a road map of your home area.
- Working with a friend, practice giving directions to one another, between different places.

6.2 THE SHOP SYSTEM

Target

* To understand that shops are businesses run for **profit**.
* To learn that businesses are **systems** with **inputs** and **outputs**.
* To collect and present data about a business system.

Neil's photo shop has to make a **profit**, so that he can make a living. Like all businesses, Neil's shop makes a profit when he sells things for more than they cost him to buy.

Neil could not continue in business if he did not have the support of other firms supplying him, together with the support of his customers.

Everything that comes into the business from outside is an **input**. **Outputs** are the opposite of inputs. Both outputs and inputs can be shown in a **systems diagram**.

A

BUSINESS SURVEY

Collector's Name	Abdul Ali
What is the name of the business?	J. Neil Fletcher
What sort is it?	A shop. Photographic.
Where is it? (location)	
What does it sell or offer? (outputs)	
What has to be brought in from outside? (inputs)	Films, frames, cameras, the photocopier. Labour - usually just Neil, his wife and mother help at busy times. Car.

Business survey sheet

B

INPUTS — FILMS, LABOUR → FLETCHER STUDIO → OUTPUTS — FILMS, SLIDES

Systems diagram

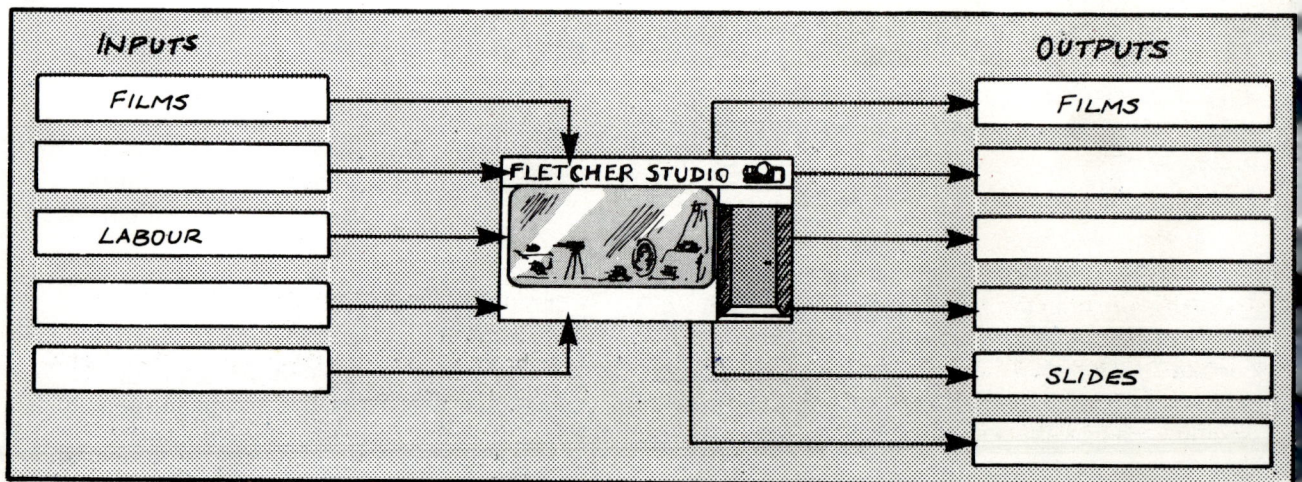

Making a Living

CORE ACTIVITIES

C

P	E	D	A	S	E	M	A	R	F	A
H	H	P	O	S	H	A	U	I	Q	D
O	C	O	P	O	S	B	L	C	S	B
T	H	P	T	D	P	M	R	B	V	A
O	O	Q	O	O	S	T	U	T	T	T
C	G	T	L	R	G	T	O	S	Q	S
O	T	D	P	E	T	R	B	F	T	E
P	I	I	T	I	C	T	A	A	G	D
I	P	T	T	P	U	L	L	P	S	I
E	K	T	O	O	D	W	T	T	H	L
S	Y	H	T	C	A	M	E	R	A	S

Wordsearch

1. **A** shows a business survey sheet for Neil's shop. It has been partly completed.
   - On a copy of **A**, write in the missing facts.
     Unit 6.1 will help you find out where Neil's shop is and what he sells.

2. **C** is a wordsearch which has eight of the shop's inputs and outputs hidden inside it.
   - Find them and write them down.
   - Make a copy of **B**.
   - Complete **B** by filling in the empty boxes. Use the words taken from the wordsearch puzzle. You will find that you will need to use some words twice.
     EXAMPLE: Films appears twice because Neil sells films that the makers sell to him.

3. Imagine a large store is coming to locate in your local town or city.
   - Describe how you think this might effect the people living there.
     (*HINT*: Think about jobs it would create and the services it would provide)
   - What would be the effect of a large store in your local town or city closing?

Neil's photo shop is a small family business. Apart from himself, the only other people who work there are his wife and his mother.

Larger shops, like the sort you would find in the high street of your local town or city, can employ lots of people.

EXTENSION ACTIVITIES

4. Look at **A** and **B** again.
   - Think about the outputs of Neil's business.
   - Design an advertisement for Neil to put in the local paper. It should show what he can offer, in a way that will make people want to use the shop.

5. Imagine you were doing the business survey shown in **A**.
   - What questions would you have asked? How would Neil have answered?
   - Do your own survey of a local business.
   - Use your findings to draw a systems diagram.

57

6.3 LOCATING A BUSINESS

Target

* To understand how some locations are better than others for making a living.
* To look at some of the different factors which help to decide where a business is located.

Locating a business means deciding where to put it.

When Neil Fletcher opened his photo shop there were two empty shops for him to choose between. One shop was on Front Street and the other on Percy Park Road. He chose the site in Percy Park Road because he thought it was the better location.

A shows where Neil's shop is located in Percy Park Road. **B** shows some of the factors Neil thought about when he made his location decision.

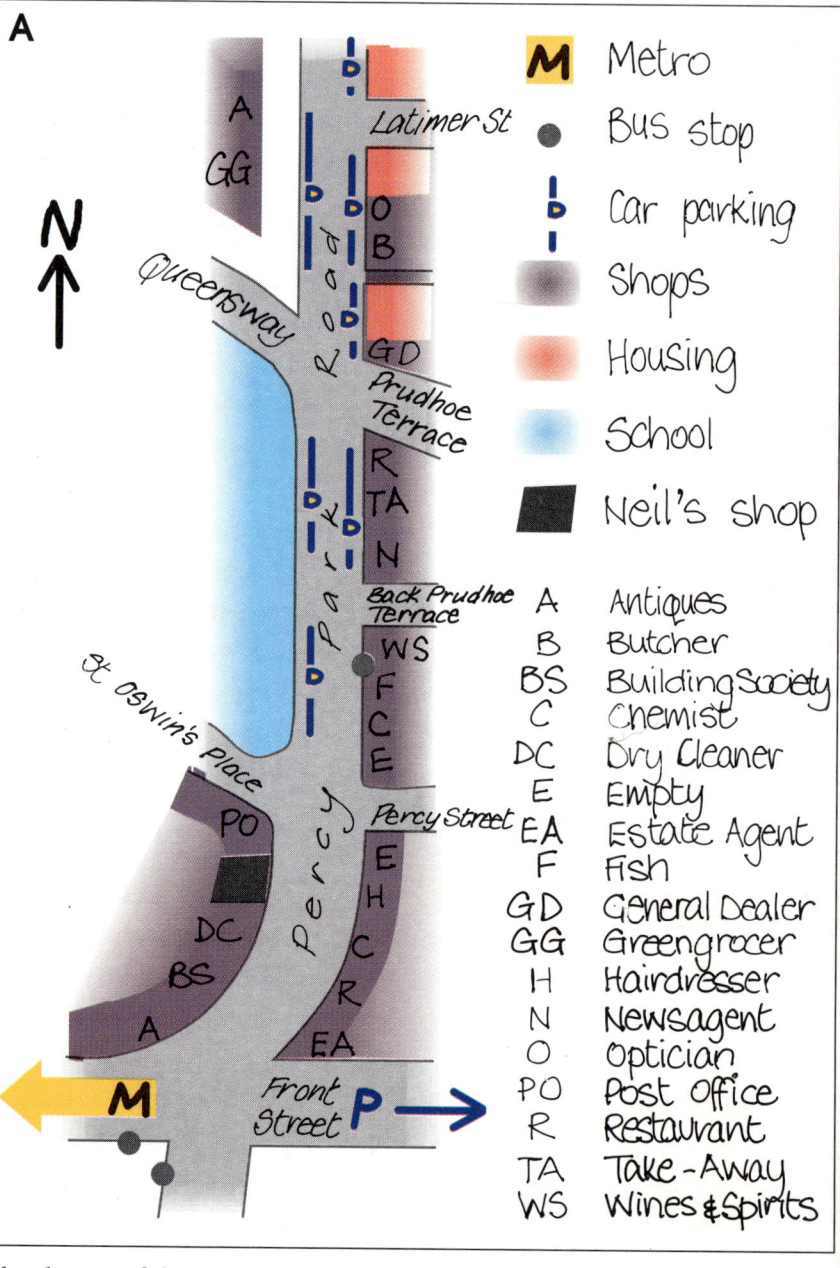

A

Map key:
- M — Metro
- Bus stop
- Car parking
- Shops
- Housing
- School
- Neil's shop

- A — Antiques
- B — Butcher
- BS — Building Society
- C — Chemist
- DC — Dry Cleaner
- E — Empty
- EA — Estate Agent
- F — Fish
- GD — General Dealer
- GG — Greengrocer
- H — Hairdresser
- N — Newsagent
- O — Optician
- PO — Post Office
- R — Restaurant
- TA — Take-Away
- WS — Wines & Spirits

Sketch map of the village end of Percy Park Road

CORE ACTIVITIES

1. Look at **A**. Some of the shops shown on the map are the sort that local people might use at least once a week.
   * Which of the following shops do you think would be used at least once a week by local people?
     newsagent antique shop greengrocer Post Office restaurant butcher estate agent
   * Make a list of all the shops in Percy Park Road that would be used this often. How many are there?

2. Imagine you are Neil.
   * Why is it important for you to have your business close to other shops that people use often?

3. Neil thinks it is a particular advantage for his shop to be close to the Post Office and the primary school.
   * Try to explain why.

4. Neil's shop is close to the junction of Percy Park Road and Front Street.
   * Why is this an advantage?

Making a Living

Neil decided to choose 8 Percy Park Road for his shop because he believes that a lot of local people pass that way every day. In his opinion not so many locals use Front Street as often.

People passing by is not enough. For Neil to make a living he has to attract people into the shop. **C** shows the front of Neil's shop.

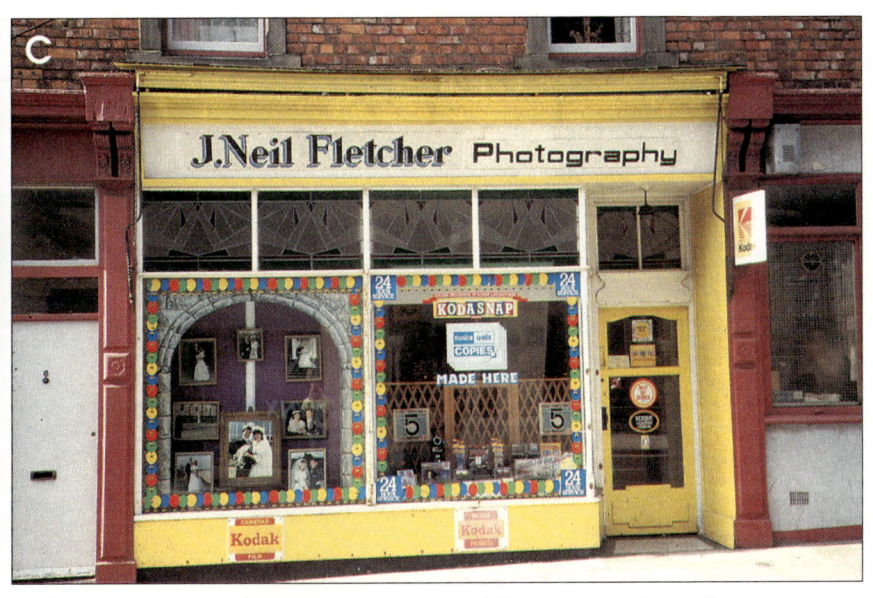

C

Neil's shop. In the window is a display of the cameras he sells

B

Location?

Close to shops
— Sub Post Office
— Primary School
— Local Shops

Easy Access

Neil's checklist - the factors in his decision

EXTENSION ACTIVITIES

5 Look at **B**.
- Write down the two main **factors** Neil thought about before choosing a site for his shop.
- Make a copy of the list.
- Complete it by filling in the evidence for Percy Park Road being easy to reach.

6 Think about your answers for Activities 1 to 4.
- Write a summary to explain why Neil chose the business location he did.

7 Using **C**:
- Make a labelled a sketch of the front of Neil's shop. Your labels should show the ways in which Neil is trying to attract customers.
  EXAMPLE: Cameras in the window attract people's attention.

8 There are two types of public transport that people can use to reach Percy Park Road.
- What are they?

9 Neil believes that Percy Park Road is busier than Front Street. This could be described as a hypothesis. Supposing you wanted to test this.
- (☞ GLOSSARY).
- Look up the word hypothesis and remind yourself what it means. (You first came across this word in Unit 3.2.)
- How would you test if it is true that more local people use Percy Park Road than Front Street?

10 Imagine you are Neil. You've just chosen the shop's location.
- Write a letter to your bank manager to explain your decision. Give as many reasons as you can.

6.4 DIFFERENT JOBS

Target

* To understand that the different jobs people do can be fitted into one of four groups.

People do a great variety of different jobs. These different jobs belong to one of four groups. The groups are shown by **A**.

Graphs can be used to present data about how many people have jobs in each group. **C** shows the jobs done by 100 people. This has been done here by using a **divided bar graph**.

A

Primary jobs.

These include farming, fishing and mining. They involve getting raw materials from the earth or sea.

Secondary jobs.

These include toolmaking, shipbuilding and weaving. They involve making goods from raw materials.

Tertiary jobs.

These include people who do work which provides a service. Examples are driver, nurse and teacher.

Quaternary jobs.

These include people who do work which involves giving information. Examples are people working in microchip industries.

CORE ACTIVITIES

1 Look at **A**. Each sketch shows one example of each of the four types of job.
 * Draw four different sketches of your own, one for each type of job.
 * Write four sentences to explain what each of the job groups are.

2 Look at **B**.
 * Make a table of the jobs in the advertisements. It should start like this:

JOB	EMPLOYER	GROUP

3 Now look at your table.
 * Which job groups are shown?
 * How many jobs from each of these groups are shown?
 * Which job groups are not shown at all?

4 Look at **C**.
 * Write down how many jobs from each group it shows.
   EXAMPLE: Number of primary jobs = 10.
 * Which group has most jobs?
 * Which group has fewest jobs?

Making a Living

B

LEGAL SECRETARIES URGENT!!!
I have a number of companies looking for high calibre, career-minded experienced secretaries in all fields of law. Salaries according to age and experience.

Earn up to and in excess of £14,000 Company perks. Call for immediate interview.

CHRISTINE BLACK
335 6148
P & R ASSOCIATES

ASSISTANT COOK
Required to work in our school kitchens, carrying out general cooking duties. Based at Preston, near Hitchin you should hold City & Guilds 706/1, ideally with some relevant experience. Working 35 hrs p.w. you will receive £3.60ph plus an excellent benefits package including a holiday retainer, uniform and meals.

To apply please contact
Sheila Brown on (0219) 6032

BARKERS RECRUITMENT SERVICES
are the country's leading recruitment agency. We currently have vacancies for telephonists. Varied duties including telex, typing and general office duties. Good company benefits.

Call Ray Bore on 77747

Tooling Service Ltd
Skilled MILLERS TOOLMAKERS & FITTERS
are required to carry out interesting and varied work for the automotive and aircraft industries.
Our rates are competitive and a bonus scheme is in operation.
Write or telephone for an interview.
Tooling Service Ltd
Tel: (0992) 2480

BELSTAR Management Services are one of the country's leading employment agencies. We currently have vacancies for ambitious, self-motivating people looking for a career in the exciting field of recruitment. For more details contact 0525 414962 now!

BRICKLAYERS and HODS WANTED
LUTON 6423

FACTORY STAFF REQUIRED
To manufacture double glazed windows and doors. Engineering experience essential.
Telephone 874 218960

AIRCRAFT FITTERS!
Long contract!
Immediate start!
Top rates.
Taskforce Emp Agy 773 94291

HAIR STYLIST REQUIRED
For busy town centre hair salon.
Tel: Becky 675465

SALARY £11,500+
Personnel Secretary. Be responsible for staff payroll. Recruit office staff to middle management. Deal with day to day staff queries. W.P. skills required. Liaison at all staff levels, good company perks offered including free flights.
Call Pauline now on
Longbottoms Recruitment Centre.
Local interviews arranged, ref 0288.

MULLENS LTD Fabricators/Welders
required with aluminium experience. Immediate start.
Contact T. Mullen on 472788

ADMINISTRATION OFFICER
Hollingsworth Products, one of the UK's leading manufacturers of sealing and bonding materials, has a vacancy for an Administration Officer. The vacancy is within the Technical Service and Development Departments, reporting directly to the Technical Service/Development Manager, providing a full secretarial and administrative back-up. The work involved is establishing new departmental systems in the areas of job feed-back and project priority, also to monitor personnel requirements. The position is full and varied and will require someone who can handle telephone enquiries in a professional and confident manner and be able to communicate at all levels. The candidate should have good shorthand and/or audio and typewriting qualifications.
Please write enclosing a full cv and salary details to:
The Personnel Officer, Hollingsworth Products, Woodside Estate, Atherstone, Warwickshire CV8 2DG

TELEPHONE 696666 EXT 277

Newspaper job advertisements

C

Divided bar chart showing Primary (blue), Secondary (green), Tertiary (light green), Quaternary (yellow)

Scale: 0 to 10 jobs

- Primary
- Secondary
- Tertiary
- Quaternary

Divided bar, showing the amount of jobs in each group

EXTENSION ACTIVITY

5 Job advertisements often appear in newspapers.
- Collect old copies of local and national newspapers.
- Read the job advertisements.
- Cut out some examples and organise them into the four different groups shown on these pages.
- You could make a display of them.
- What can you say about the number of jobs available in each group?
- Do some types of job pay more than others? If so, which group(s) do they belong to?

61

6.5 FARMING IN THE UK

Target

* To understand that farms are businesses.
* To look at two different types of farming in the UK.
* To understand where some of the main farming types in the UK are to be found and how they are changing.

In the UK farmers sell the crops they have grown or the animals they have reared, for cash. They do this because they wish to make a profit. Farms are businesses.

Other people make a living on a farm as well. The farmer may employ farm workers to help on the farm. Often other members of the farmer's family make their living on the farm too.

A

The Young family and their farm - Kite's Nest

Four other people also work on the farm: one full-time and three part-time

CORE ACTIVITIES

1 Look at **A**.
   - What is the name of this farm?
   - How many people make a full-time living from the farm?
   - How many people make a part-time living from the farm?

2 Look at **B**.
   - Copy and complete the following:
     In the UK, hill farms are mostly found in the north and _____ on _____ areas where the **climate** is often _____ and _____. One region where hill farms are found is _____.

3 Using the key on **B**:
   - List four different types of farm found in the UK.
   - Match each of the four types of farming, below, to the correct meaning (☞ GLOSSARY):

     - **Hill farm**   a farm where vegetables, fruit or flowers are grown.
     - **Dairy farm**   a farm where crops are grown.
     - **Market garden**   an upland farm, usually where sheep are kept.
     - **Arable farm**   a farm where cows are reared for milk.

     EXAMPLE: Hill farm is an upland farm, usually where sheep are kept.

4 Use the labels from **B** to complete the table:

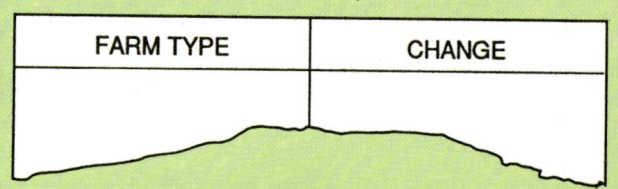

FARM TYPE	CHANGE

5 Using **C** and **D**:
   - Describe what a hill farm is like.
     (*HINT*: Think about the shape of the land and how it is used, as well as about fields and buildings on the farm)
   - Try to explain why the improved land and the buildings are on the valley floor.
     (*HINT*: Think about the soil and the weather)

6 **E** is a data table. Use it to:
   - Draw a bar graph to show the land use of the farm.
   - Which of these farm types do you think this farm is?
     - hill farm
     - dairy farm
     - market garden
     - arable farm
   - Suggest a region of the UK where such a farm could be found.

Making a Living

B

Hill farming - mostly in cold, damp uplands of the north and west; difficult to work; hill farms are being abandonned.

Arable farming - mostly on flatter areas of fertile soil and less rainfall; hedges between fields are being removed to allow for machinery

Market gardening - mostly in sheltered, warmer places which have easy access to urban markets; less chemicals being used and more organic produce being grown

Dairy farming - mostly on low lying places, often with a damp climate where grass grows well; more mechanised than it used to be

Mixed farming

Cattle

Some UK farming regions

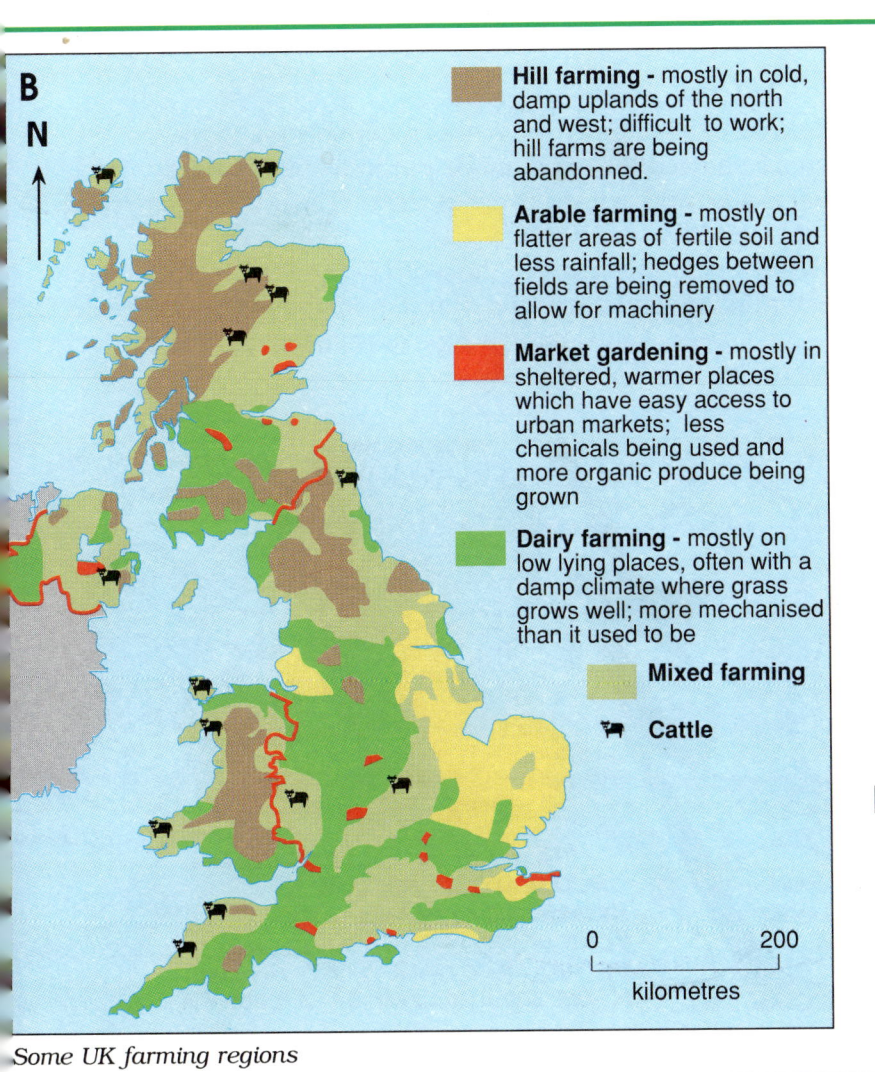

C

A hill farm

D

River
Road
200 — Contour (metres)
Field boundaries
Farm buildings
Inbye land - improved grass on the valley floor
Intake land - fenced unimproved grazing land
Open fell land - common rough grazing

Hill farm land in the Lake District

E

LAND USE	AREA (ha)
Barley	13.5
Wheat	12.5
Farm yard and buildings	1.2
Sugar beet	12.0
Vegetables	5.5
Pasture land	8.5

1 hectare (ha) = 10 000 m^2

Farm land use data

EXTENSION ACTIVITIES

7 Look back at Activity 3.
- Write your own descriptions of where the following types of farm are mostly found in the UK:
  - dairy farms
  - market gardens
  - arable farms

8 Try to find out about another farm.
- What type of farm is it?
- How is the land on it used?
- How many people make a living from the farm?

63

7.1 WORKPLACES

Target

* To understand that work is not always a job.
* To look at different sorts of workplace.
* To collect and present data about people's working days.

Workplaces are simply the places where people work. Unit 6.5 showed that jobs can be put into one of four groups but what is a *job* and is it the same as *work*? The activities on these pages may help you decide.

Ask most people to explain the word *job* and they will probably say that it involves work and that it is something you get paid for. Do you agree? Think about a type of *work* that people do not get paid for. Is it still a *job*?

A

I'M IN ADVERTISING. HOW ABOUT YOU?

OH, I DON'T HAVE A JOB - I'M JUST A HOUSEWIFE.

SO WHAT DO YOU DO THEN?

ME - I'M A PROFESSIONAL HOUSEWIFE. MY JOB RESPONSIBILITY HAS JUST GONE UP NOW WE'VE MOVED, AND I'VE HAD ANOTHER BABY. I'M NOW ON THE EQUIVALENT OF £9,000 P.A.

Housework is work

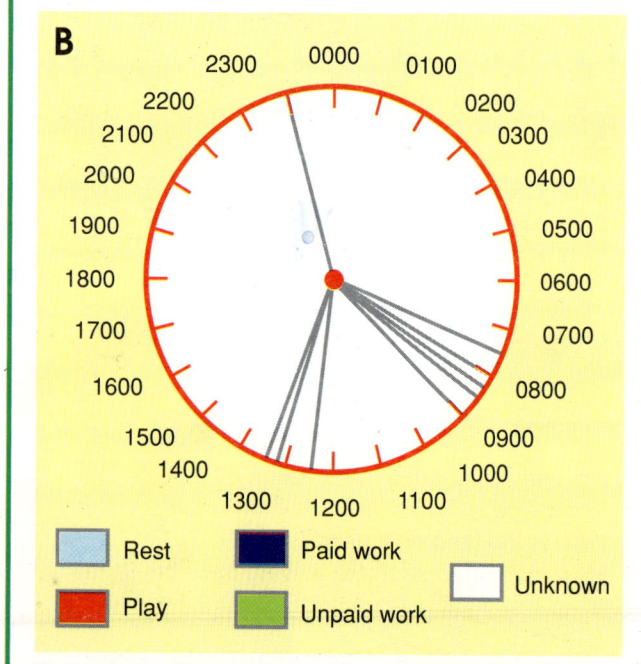

B

Rest, Paid work, Play, Unpaid work, Unknown

Time clock, showing part of a woman's day

CORE ACTIVITIES

1 Look at **A**.
* Copy out each of these statements. Write true or false after each one.
  - Both these women do a paid job.
  - Both these women work.
  - Ruth does not think much of what a housewife does.
  - Lucy does not have a workplace.
  - Housework is not real work.
  - Houses are workplaces.
* Copy and complete the table in **D**.
* Use your completed table to colour in a copy of the time clock shown in **B**.

2 Using **D** to help you:
* Make a table for your day.
* Present the results as a time clock.
* Add up the number of hours you spend working, resting and playing.
* Make a table and a bar graph to show your results.

Places for Work

Workplaces

D

TIME OF DAY	JOB	PAID/UNPAID?
7.30 am	Cook breakfast	
8.00 am	Wash up	
8.15 am	Make beds	
8.30 am	Get children ready for school	
9.00 am	Work at shop	
12.30 pm	Go shopping for family	
1.15 pm	Snack lunch	
1.30 pm	Work at shop	
	etc.	

A day's work

3 There is a saying, "A woman's work is never done".
 ● Do you agree?
 ● Explain your answer.

4 Look at **C**. It shows some different workplaces.
 ● Make a list of six workplaces you can see in **C**.

5 A school is a workplace!
 ● Make a list of at least five types of worker in a school.

6 Just about every sort of building you can think of is a workplace for somebody.
 ● Think of as many different ones as you can. Here are some starters:
 factory   docks   farm   cafe   shop   garage   house   church
 ● Hide these and as many more as you can think of in a wordsearch.
 ● Challenge someone to solve your wordsearch. Ask them to write down the work people do in each place.
 (*HINT*: Ask them to think of more than one sort of work for each place)

EXTENSION ACTIVITIES

7 Ask other people about their day.
 ● Record the data in tables like the one in **D**.
 ● Draw time clocks to present the data.

8 Imagine you are the woman whose morning is shown by **D** and **B**. You have just heard a man on television say that women do not do real work like men do.
 ● Write a letter to the producer of the programme. Say why you object. Tell her about your mornings.

9 For a small place you know, a street, a housing estate, or a village:
 ● Do a survey of workplaces.
 ● List them.
 ● Draw a sketch map to show where they are.
 ● Make a bar graph of the different types you find.

65

7.2 MERSEYSIDE

Target

* To understand that there is a pattern to where workplaces are usually found.
* To learn the names and locations of conurbations in the United Kingdom.

The most famous place in Merseyside is the city of Liverpool (**A**). There are many different workplaces in cities like Liverpool.

Liverpool

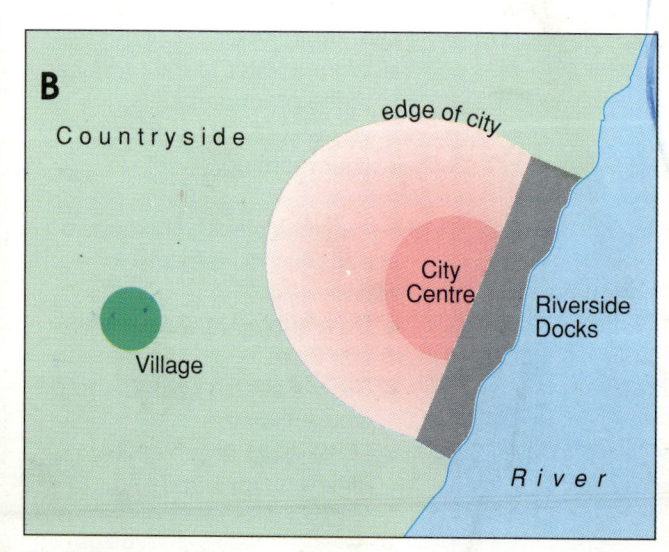

Workplaces pattern

CORE ACTIVITIES

1 Look carefully at photo **A**. On the photo are letters A to E.
   - Match each letter to one of these numbered features:
     - River Mersey
     - Central Business District
     - Dual carriageway road
     - Urban renewal area
     - Ship in dock
     EXAMPLE: A = 4 Urban renewal area.

2 Look again at **A**.
   - Write down one piece of evidence from the photo to support each of these statements about Liverpool:
     - Liverpool is a port.
     - Liverpool's roads have a lot of traffic.
     - Liverpool is a big city.
     - The docks of Liverpool are not very busy.
     - Parts of Liverpool have been renewed.
     EXAMPLE: We can see Liverpool is a port because there are docks along the riverside.

3 Here is a list of workplaces:
   - Copy out this list of workplaces.
     - Department store
     - Farm
     - Office block
     - Factory
     - Hotel
     - Mine
     - Airport
     - Nuclear power station
     - Bank
     - A building site
   - Put a tick next to the workplaces that you would expect to find in the CENTRE of a city.

4 **B** is a sketch map of a region.
   - Make a copy of **B**.
   - Mark on your copy a place where you would expect to find each of the workplaces listed in Activity 3. (*HINT*: You will need to use a key)
   - Choose three of the workplaces from the map you have made.
   - For each one write a sentence to explain why you would expect to find it in the place you have marked.

Places for Work

Liverpool and other towns beside the River Mersey have grown in size so much that they have joined together. They have created a large built-up area. An urban area that is made up of towns joined together is called a conurbation. Merseyside is a conurbation.

5 **C** shows a map of the Merseyside conurbation. It also shows that there are several other conurbations in the United Kingdom.
- Copy and complete the key for **C** by using these clues to match each place to its letter:
  - The River Mersey flows through the middle.
  - Liverpool Bay, where the Mersey goes.
  - Liverpool is on the east bank of the river where it is narrowest.
  - Crosby, on the same side as Liverpool, at the north end.
  - Garston, next to the airport.
  - Bootle, between Liverpool and Crosby.
  - Kirkby, in the north east corner.
  - Birkenhead, opposite Liverpool.
  - Wallasey, north of Birkenhead.

6 There is a scale on the map.
- Use it to find the straight line distances between these pairs of places, giving your answer to the nearest kilometre:
  - Liverpool and the Airport
  - Kirkby and Liverpool
  - Wallasey and Garston
  - Garston and Crosby
- Write down the directions of each of these places from Liverpool:
  - Kirkby
  - Garston
  - Birkenhead
  - Liverpool Bay.
- Make a table to show the main city in each of the seven conurbations shown.

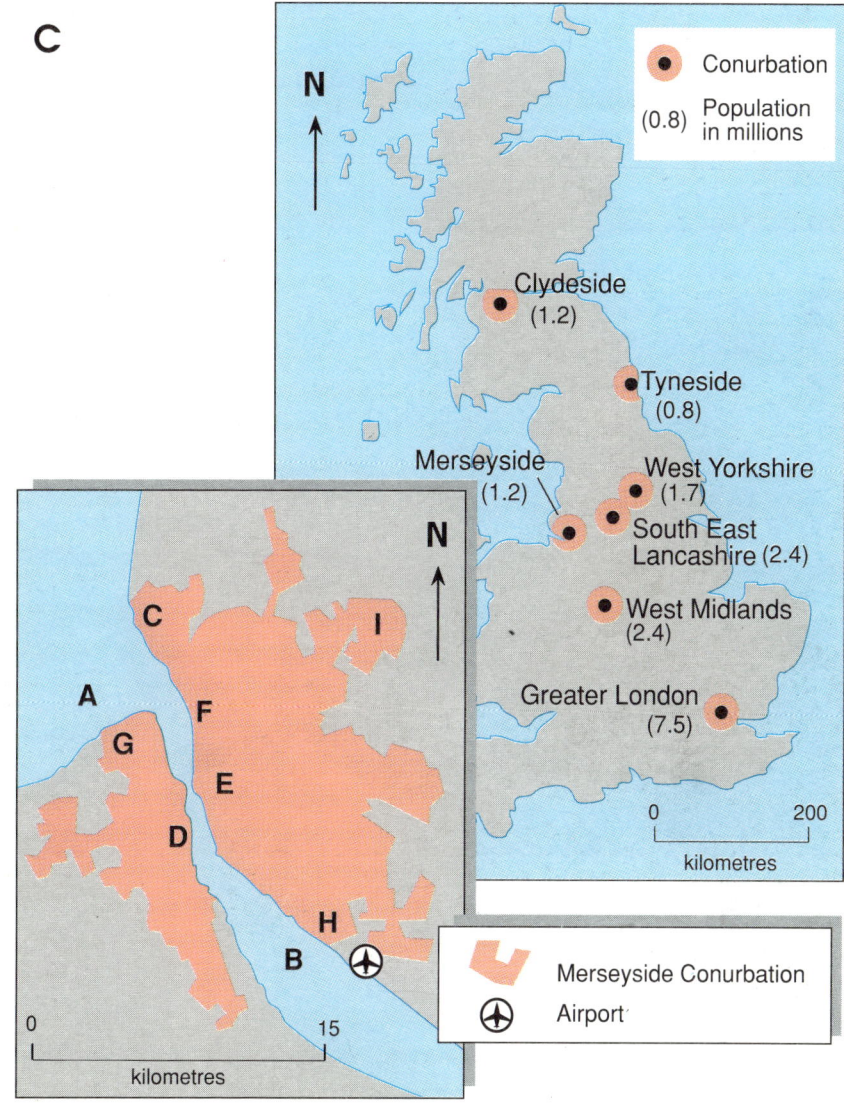

C

Conurbations

Key:
- Conurbation
- (0.8) Population in millions

Clydeside (1.2)
Tyneside (0.8)
Merseyside (1.2)
West Yorkshire (1.7)
South East Lancashire (2.4)
West Midlands (2.4)
Greater London (7.5)

0 — 200 kilometres

0 — 15 kilometres

Merseyside Conurbation
Airport

EXTENSION ACTIVITIES

7 **C** also shows the population of Britain's conurbations in millions.
- Make a table to record these data and a graph to present them.

8 Look closely at the location of the conurbations shown on the map, **C**.
- Why do you think that there are no conurbations in the north of Scotland, Wales and in the South West?
(*HINT*: Use an atlas to help you answer this question)

67

7.3 BRUNSWICK BUSINESS PARK

Target

* To learn what **Business Parks** are.
* To understand that Business Parks may include several types of business.
* To compare a picture and a plan.

Brunswick **Business Park** was created by Merseyside Development Corporation. It is located on Liverpool's waterfront and has been built on the site of two old docks. These were filled in and their old warehouses made into factory units.

One of the main aims of Brunswick is to attract new businesses to the area and provide work for the people of Merseyside. Brunswick Business Park is very accessible. It is only 3 minutes' drive from the centre of Liverpool and 15 minutes from the airport. Several motorways are also within easy reach.

A

Brunswick Business Park

CORE ACTIVITIES

1 Here are some sentences about what can be seen in **A**.
   * Use words from the list at the end to finish the sentences.
     - Brunswick Business Park is next to the River _____ .
     - It is near the city of _____ .
     - The site is _____ .
     - The buildings are _____ and made of _____ .
     - To reach each building there is a service _____ through the middle of the _____ Park.
     - The buildings are big enough to fit delivery _____ .
     - There is plenty of space for each factory _____ .
     unit   Liverpool   long   Mersey   lorries
     brick   Business   road   flat   parking

2 **C** shows three businesses in the Brunswick Business Park.
   * Look carefully at these photos.
   * Describe what work is being carried out in each.
   * Which photo shows an example of secondary type industry?
   * What type of industry are the other two businesses?

3 Businesses which make things are called **manufacturing industries**.
   * Which photo in **C** shows a manufacturing industry?
   * Are manufacturing jobs primary, secondary or tertiary?

Places for Work

B

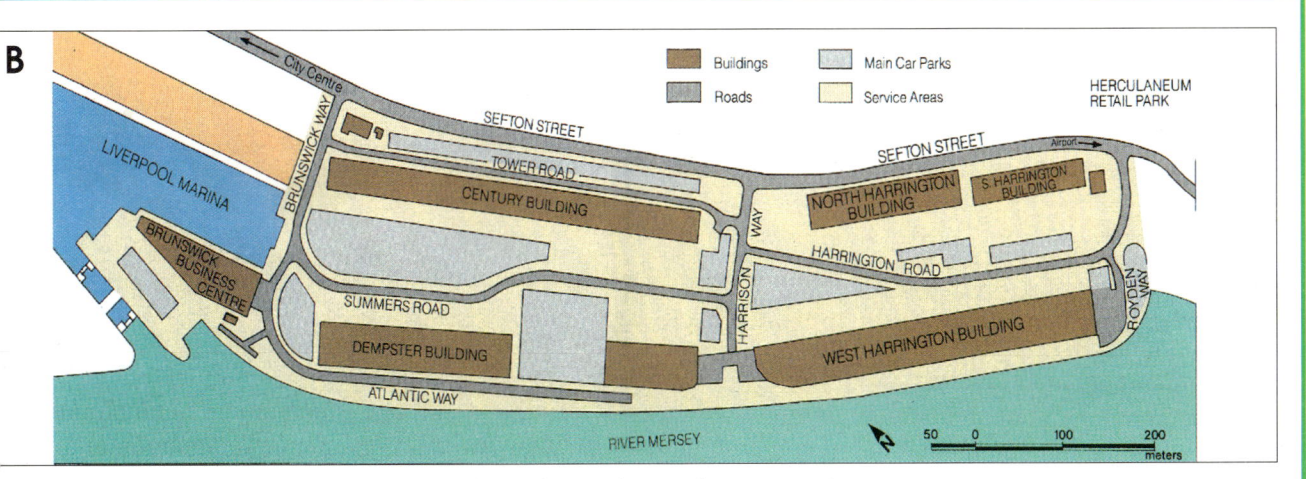

[Map legend: Buildings, Roads, Main Car Parks, Service Areas]

A *plan of the Brunswick Business Park. Why is this a plan and not a map?*

C

Brunswick businesses

4 Here is a list of some of the businesses on Brunswick Park, together with what they do:
   - Platers: make coatings for metals
   - Food processors: smoke salmon
   - Meat packers: package poultry (chickens, etc.)
   - Chandlers: supply ships with food and other needs
   - Printers: print paper
   - Car dealers: sell cars
   - Distributors: send goods round the country in lorries
   - BBC: make television programmes

   • How many of these businesses on Brunswick Business Park have mainly tertiary jobs?
   (*HINT*: Look back to Unit 6.5)

5 Using the information from Activities 3 and 4:
   • Make a bar graph to show the number of secondary and tertiary businesses on Brunswick Business Park. Your answers to Activities 3 and 4 have given you enough information.

6 Look at **A** and the plan **B** together.
   • The building with the tower is called the Century Building. What is the name of the road through the middle of **A**?
   • Name two of the buildings on the left of **A**.
   • Which way was the artist looking when **A** was drawn?

A plan shows the exact shape and size of every detail, buildings, car parks, roads, everything.
A map uses symbols to show details. **C** from Unit 7.2 is a map. It uses letters and circles to show places.

EXTENSION ACTIVITY

7 Use this book to find more examples of plans and maps.
   • Make a table to show which of them are maps and which are plans.

69

7.4 WHY CHOOSE BRUNSWICK?

Target

* To see how Business Parks can bring new jobs to a place.
* To look at some of the needs of industry.
* To understand that manufacturing industries are systems.

Businesses bring jobs. Liverpool is an area of relatively high unemployment, so bringing jobs to Merseyside is important.

Brunswick Business Park is run by Merseyside Development Corporation. It has used public money to set it up and to try to persuade industry to come to Merseyside.

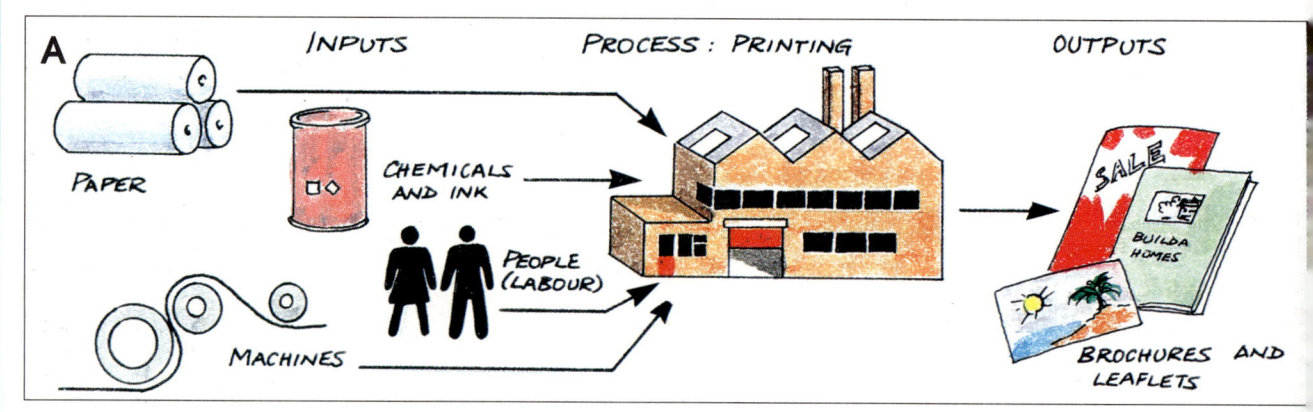

A

A systems diagram for a printing business

Like all industries, the printing industry has a system. A printing firm making colour brochures and leaflets is thinking about coming to Brunswick Business Park, if it can provide the company with what it needs. The decision whether or not to go to Brunswick will be taken by the board of the company. **B** shows a Board Meeting. This group of people is in charge of the firm. One of the most important things the Board members have to consider before making their decision is **access**. (☞ GLOSSARY) **C** is a map showing the accessibility of Brunswick Business Park. In other words, how easy it is to reach.

CORE ACTIVITIES

1 **A** is a diagram showing what goes into and what comes out of a printing business.
   * List four inputs and two outputs of the firm.
   * Write two sentences to explain what the words input and output mean.

2 Inputs can be materials. Outputs are made from such materials.
   * Which two materials are shown by **A**?

3 **A** is called a systems diagram.
   * Draw systems diagrams for these factories:
     - a chocolate factory using cocoa, sugar, milk and water
     - a jeans factory using dye, cotton, thread, zips, metal buttons and rivets
   Both industries use machines and **labour** too.

4 Below is a list of roads, together with their destinations. At present, they are wrongly paired.
   * Use **B** to help you pair them correctly.
     - A41   goes to   Manchester
     - M53   goes to   the M6 South
     - A561   goes to   Chester
     - M58   goes to   Widnes
     - A580   goes to   the M56 South
     - M62   goes to   the M6 North

5 Some of the links on **B** have not been built. They are only proposed and may be built in the future.
   * Make a sketch map version of **B** showing the transport links that are there today.
   * Make a table to show the numbers of roads, motorways, airports and railways in the area around Brunswick Business Park today and in the future.

Places for Work

B

LINKS WITHIN MERSEYSIDE DEVELOPMENT AREA
- Development area (hatched)
- Commuter railway (dashed)
- Motorway (thick blue)
- Main road
- Proposed road (dotted)

Access map

C

"THE FACTOR THAT MATTERS MOST IS ACCESS. THERE ARE EXCELLENT ROADS TO GET OUR INPUTS AND SEND OUR OUTPUTS AWAY TO BE SOLD"

"ELECTRICITY, GAS, WATER, TELEPHONE ALL THE BASIC SERVICES ARE ALREADY LAID ON"

"THE RENTS ARE NOT TOO MUCH"

"THERE ARE OTHER FIRMS MOVING INTO THE PARK WE COULD SELL OUR BROCHURES TO THEM"

"BRUNSWICK IS NEAR ENOUGH TO THE CITY FOR US TO HAVE A LABOUR-FORCE. THERE'S A TRAINING CENTRE TOO SO WE'LL BE ABLE TO FIND SKILLED PEOPLE"

"YOU HAVE TO THINK ABOUT SECURITY THESE DAYS. THERE IS A PROPER FENCE ROUND THE BUSINESS PARK AND THE GATES ARE MANNED"

"ENVIRONMENT IS IMPORTANT. THIS PLACE IS BY THE RIVER. THERE ARE LEISURE AND SHOPPING FACILITIES NEARBY AND THE BUILDINGS HAVE BEEN MADE TO LOOK VERY GOOD."

D

Brunswick Business Park entrance

6 Read the comments made by the members of the board in **C**.
- How many factors have they discussed?
- Make a list of these.
- Which factor is said to matter most?
- Give two reasons why it is the most important factor.

7 **D** shows a lorry from Sheffield arriving at the Brunswick Business Park entrance.
- Find Sheffield on a map in an atlas.
- Plot Sheffield and Liverpool on an outline map and add the places named on **B**. You can use a key if you wish.
- Which mountains does the lorry have to cross between Sheffield and Liverpool?
- Label them on your map.

EXTENSION ACTIVITY

8 Think about how the entrance sign to Brunswick Business Park could be improved to make it more eye-catching.
- Redesign the entrance sign to advertise Brunswick Business Park. It should be colourful and say what is good about the Park for industry. The idea is to attract firms to come to Brunswick Business Park. Include something that symbolises the Park so that people will not forget it.

71

7.5 INDUSTRIES AND REGIONS

Target

* To realise that manufacturing industries can be classed as being '**heavy**' or '**light**' **industries**.
* To look at the special location of some industries.
* To learn the location of major industrial regions in the UK.
* To understand the reasons for the growth of the North-West industrial region of England.

Manufacturing industries make all sorts of goods. Everything from a packet of sweets to an aeroplane. From this book to a video-recorder.

There are a very large number of manufacturing industries and these can be split into two main groups. These two groups are **heavy industries** and **light industries**.

Different industries are also found in different sorts of locations. **A** shows some examples of different industries that need to be in special sorts of places. It also shows some of the differences between heavy and light industries.

A

HEAVY INDUSTRIES
- make goods that weigh a lot
- sell to industry mostly
- are usually traditional
- are often in decline

Example: Shipbuilding

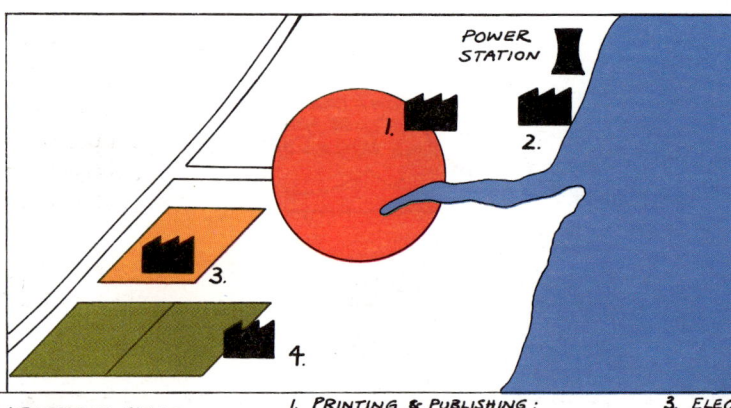

LIGHT INDUSTRIES
- make goods that weigh little
- sell to consumers a lot
- are usually modern
- are often growing

Example: Electronics

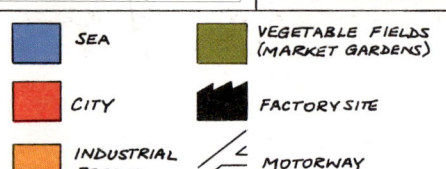

Legend:
- SEA
- CITY
- INDUSTRIAL ESTATE
- VEGETABLE FIELDS (MARKET GARDENS)
- FACTORY SITE
- MOTORWAY

1. PRINTING & PUBLISHING: Market Location (close to city where there are lots of people to sell to)
2. ALUMINIUM WORKS: Power Location (aluminium smelting uses lots of electricity)
3. ELECTRICAL GOODS: Transport Location (Components are brought by motorway from different places)
4. FOOD FREEZING: Materials Location (vegetables have to be frozen near fields so that they don't go off)

Locations for industries

CORE ACTIVITIES

1 **A** gives information about "light" and "heavy" industries.
   - Use it to help you finish each of these statements about types of industry. Each sentence has to end with 'light industry' or 'heavy industry'.
     - Making a product that weighs a lot is _____ industry.
     - Goods that do not weigh much are the products of _____ industry.
     - People buy **consumer** goods. They are made by _____ industry.
     - Factories often buy big machines. Industrial machinery is made by _____ industry.
     - Most traditional industries are _____ industries.
     - Industries that are dying are often _____ industries.
     - Electronics is a _____ industry.

2 **A** shows the special sorts of location that some industries need. Use the information on **A** to fill in a copy of this table.
   It shows four types of location.
   The first line has been completed to show you how.

Industry	Type of location	Description	Reason
Food	Materials	Close to gardens	Vegetables have to be frozen close to the fields so they

Places for Work

B shows the parts of the UK which are most important for manufacturing industry.

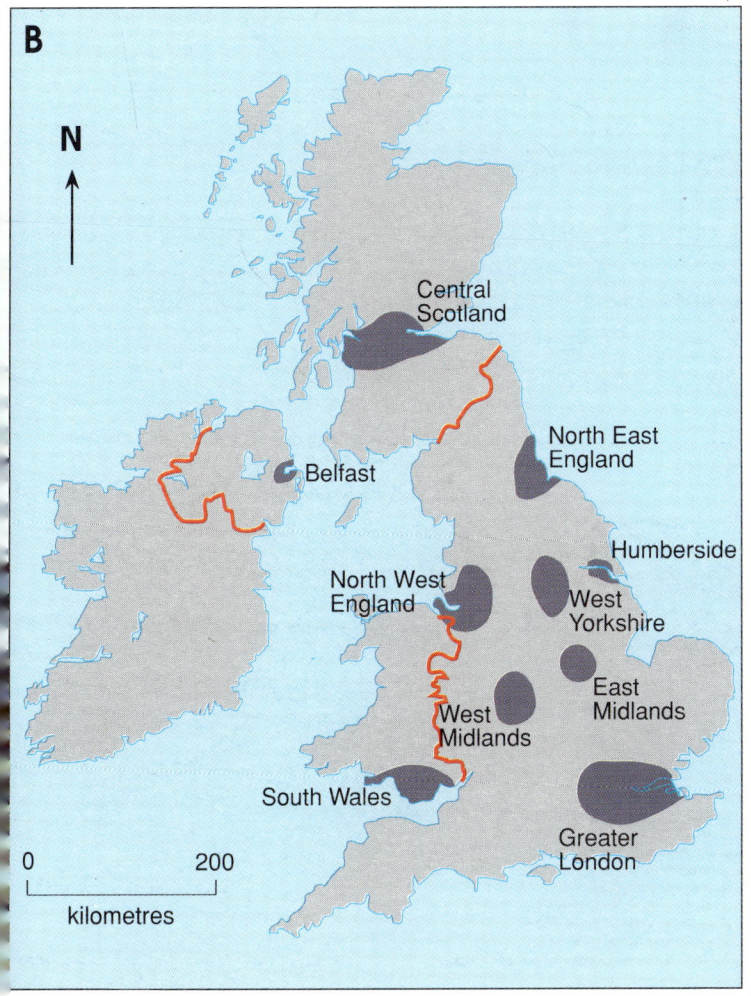

B

Major industrial regions in the UK

C

Factor	Effect on region
Coal	Coal used to make steam power for machines of early cotton industry. Chemical industry uses coal.
Salt	Salt mined in Cheshire. Important raw material in chemical industry.
Rivers	Water from rivers was important for industry. Industries use rivers to dump their waste.
Port	Raw cotton, crude oil, chemicals imported through Liverpool. Exports of finished goods – cotton clothes and so on. Later, foreign competition caused decline of cotton industry.
Rail	Liverpool – Manchester Railway (built in 1830s) helped cotton industry grow in Manchester.
Canal	Manchester Ship Canal (opened 1894) let large ships sail into Manchester.
Links	Chemical industry could sell soap, bleach and dyes to cotton industry.

3 Look at **B**.
- Which industrial region includes Merseyside?
- Copy and complete this table:

INDUSTRIAL REGION	CONURBATION

(*HINT*: Use **C** on page 67 to help you and remember, not every industrial region has a conurbation)

4 Using **C**:
- Explain why the North-West industrial region has developed.

EXTENSION ACTIVITIES

5 Try to find out about industries in your area. Perhaps you have an **industrial estate** close by.
- What sort of industries are there?
- How many are 'light' and how many are 'heavy' industries?
- What sorts of location do they have?
- Write a report on what you discover.

6 Try to find out about the growth of the major industrial region closest to where you live.
- Make a chart like the one in this unit, **C**, for your industrial region.
(*HINT*: The library is a useful source of information)

8.1 A CITY CENTRE - NORWICH

Target

* To investigate a city centre shopping street.
* To see how often people use city centre shops.
* To make a divided bar graph.

The historic city of Norwich is the most important place in the county of Norfolk. **A** is a photo of part of the city centre.
Like many older cities Norwich has lots of narrow little streets. Some of these have been pedestrianised. This means that traffic is not allowed, and so there is more room for people to shop safely.

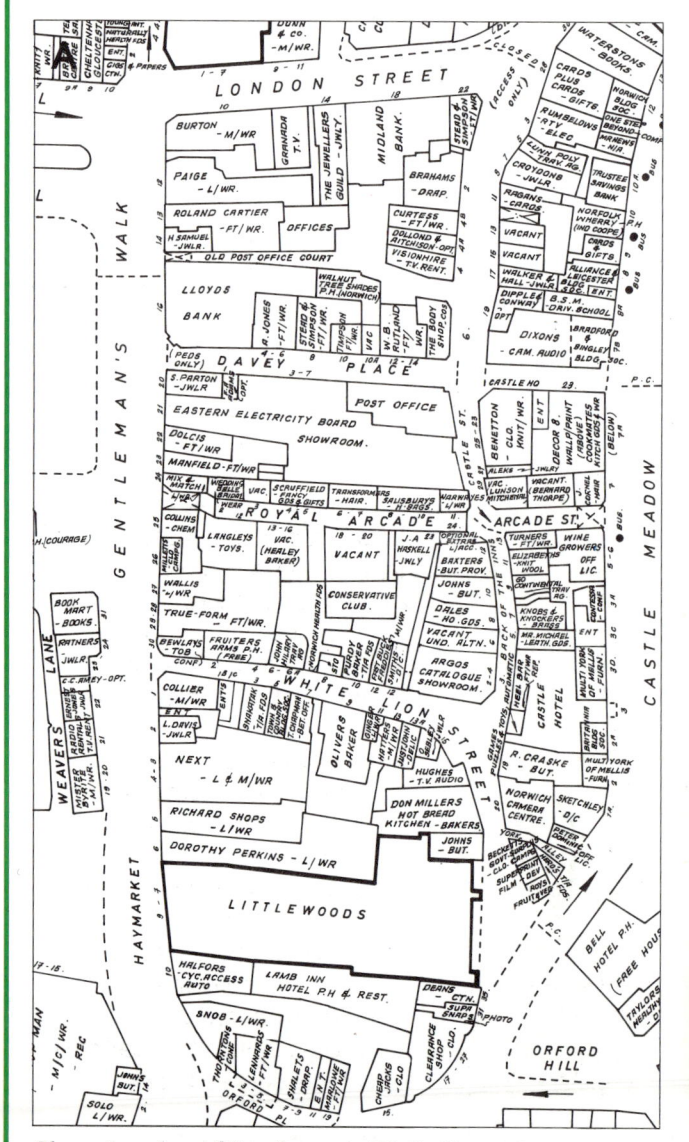

Shopping plan of Gentleman's Walk, Norwich

CORE ACTIVITIES

1 Look at **A** and **B** together. The buildings in **A** are on **B** as well.
  - Find them and then decide if each of these statements is true or false:
    - The main street on the photograph is called Gentleman's Walk.
    - Lloyds Bank is at number 16.
    - Number 22 is the electricity showroom.
    - The narrow street on the photograph is called White Lion Street.
    - The camera was pointing west.
    - The jeweller's shop has changed its name.

2 The narrow street beside the jeweller's is pedestrianised.
  - What does that mean?
  - Write a sentence to explain why you think some city centre streets are pedestrianised.

3 **A** is a plan showing some of the shops. Plans like this show how the ground floors of buildings are used.
   Imagine walking down Gentleman's Walk from Burton's to Littlewoods.
  - Which direction are you going?
  - How far is it?
  - Make a list of the shops you would pass on your left. Record the name of the shop, its number and what it sells. **C** shows how to start.

4

SHOP TYPES	NUMBER	HOW OFTEN USED

- Make a three column table like this.
- In the first column list these shop types:
  shoe clothes department store food jewellers specialist store household goods others
- Use the second column to record how many shops of each type you would pass. You only need to count the shops on the side of Gentleman's Walk that you are going along.
- The third column is for you to show how often you think people use that type of shop. Write 'very often' if you think people use that type nearly every day. If you think they use it only once a week or less, write 'only sometimes'.

Going Shopping

B

Norwich city centre

C

Name Sharon Rogers	Place Gentleman's Walk Norwich	
Shop name	Number	Sells
Burton	10	Clothes (men)

Shop survey

EXTENSION ACTIVITY

5 You can now use these data to draw two graphs:
- Draw a bar graph to show how many shops there are of each type.
- Make a divided bar graph to show the number of shops that are used very often compared with the number that are used only sometimes. To make your bar, follow these steps:
  - count the number of shops between Burton's and Littlewoods
  - make the bar 1 centimetre wide and let each shop be a block 0.5 centimetres long
  - count up the number of shops that are used very often
  - colour in the same number of blocks in the bar
  - make a key

6 Using your graphs:
- Say whether these hypotheses are true or not:
  - The most common types of shop in Gentleman's Walk are shoe shops.
  - There are no food shops in Gentleman's Walk.
  - Most shops in Gentleman's Walk are shops that people use very often.
- Write at least one sentence to explain your answers.

7 Apply what you have learned about investigating a shopping street to one you know.
- Collect and record the same sets of data.
- Make the same types of graph and write about what they show.
- Your conclusion should answer these questions:
  - What are the main shop types?
  - How often are most shops used?
  - Are some shops next to others of the same type?
  - How similar are your findings to the shop patterns of Gentleman's Walk?

8.2 DIFFERENT SHOPS

Target

* To investigate if there are patterns to the locations of city shops.

There are many different sorts and sizes of shop, from the local corner shop to the city centre department store. People use some shops daily but visit others only sometimes. Some shops sell only one special thing, others sell many different goods.

In cities, different types of shop are usually found in different sorts of place. Corner shops are on street corners all over the city except for the city centre. They are located close to people's homes.

C lists the supermarkets, department stores and music shops of Norwich (music shops are one sort of specialist shop). After each shop is its grid reference on the street map of Norwich (**D**).

CORE ACTIVITIES

1 Look at the pictures in **A**.
  - Sketch each one and match it with one of these labels: corner shop   department store   specialist shop   supermarket
  - Complete each of these sentences with one of the four shop type names from above:
    - A big city centre shop that sells lots of different things is a _____.
    - A shop that sells only computers is a _____.
    - People often buy their everyday food from the _____.
    - To buy their weekly groceries, many people visit a _____.

2 You will need a copy of the table, **B**.
  - For each type of shop, put ticks in the boxes that best describe that shop. The corner shop has been done for you as an example.

Four shops

B Shop type	Size			Sells		Visited		
	big	medium	small	one thing	many things	daily	weekly	rarely
Corner shop			✓		✓	✓		
Supermarket								
Specialist shop								
Department store								

Comparison of shop types

Going Shopping

C

Supermarkets	Department stores	Music shops
Sainsbury (C1)	Bonds (C6)	Andy's Records (B4)
Sainsbury (B7)	BHS (B7)	Back's Records (C4)
Tesco (B5)	Butchers (C4)	Cooke's Orchestral (B4)
	Habitat (C5)	Ives Records (B5)
	Jarrold & Sons (C5)	Lizard Records (B4)
	Littlewoods (C5)	Prelude Records (B5)
	Marks & Spencer (C6)	St. George's Music Shop (C3)
	Co-op (B7)	

Location of three types of shop in Norwich

D

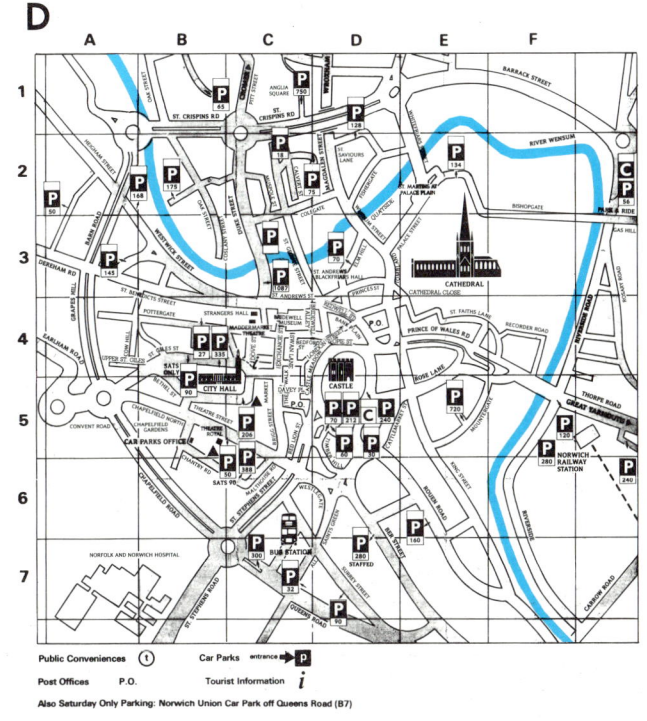

Street map of Norwich

Activities 3-6 are steps in finding out if certain shops are found in certain places in a city. They make up an enquiry.

3 Use **C** and **D** to do these tasks:
- Make a copy of the grid from **D**. It has 6 squares along and 7 squares down.
- On your grid colour the 4 city centre squares red.
- Colour the squares on the edge of the city centre orange.
- Colour the rest of the squares yellow.
- Make a key to show what the three colours mean.

4 Using **C**:
- Make a list of the supermarkets and their grid references.
- Invent a symbol for a supermarket and draw it in each of the squares on your grid where there is a supermarket.

5 Look at **C** again.
- Repeat Activity 4 for department stores and again for music shops.

EXTENSION ACTIVITIES

6 Use the map you have made to help you think about these hypotheses:
- Department stores are always found in city centres.
- Supermarkets are always found outside city centres.
- Specialist shops are scattered all over the city.
- For each hypothesis, copy it and say if you agree or disagree.
- Write at least a sentence to say why.

7 Look at your answer to Activity 6. Think about these questions:
- What did you say about specialist shops?
- Did you really have enough information to decide? If not, why not?

8 Read this unit again.
- Apply the method you have used in this unit to test this hypothesis, "Most car parks are on the edge of the city centre".
(*HINT*: Follow the steps in Activities 3-6 very carefully)

8.3 OUT OF TOWN

Target

* To understand that more out of town shopping places are being developed.
* To learn that access to these shopping places is important for their success.
* To understand people's different views about out of town shopping.

Outside many cities new shopping places are being developed. In 1988 Tesco opened a superstore on the edge of the city of Newcastle-upon-Tyne.

For Tesco to make a profit from the superstore, it needs a lot of people to buy goods there. It is important that the superstore is easy to reach. To make the access even better, Tesco laid on free buses to take people to its superstore.

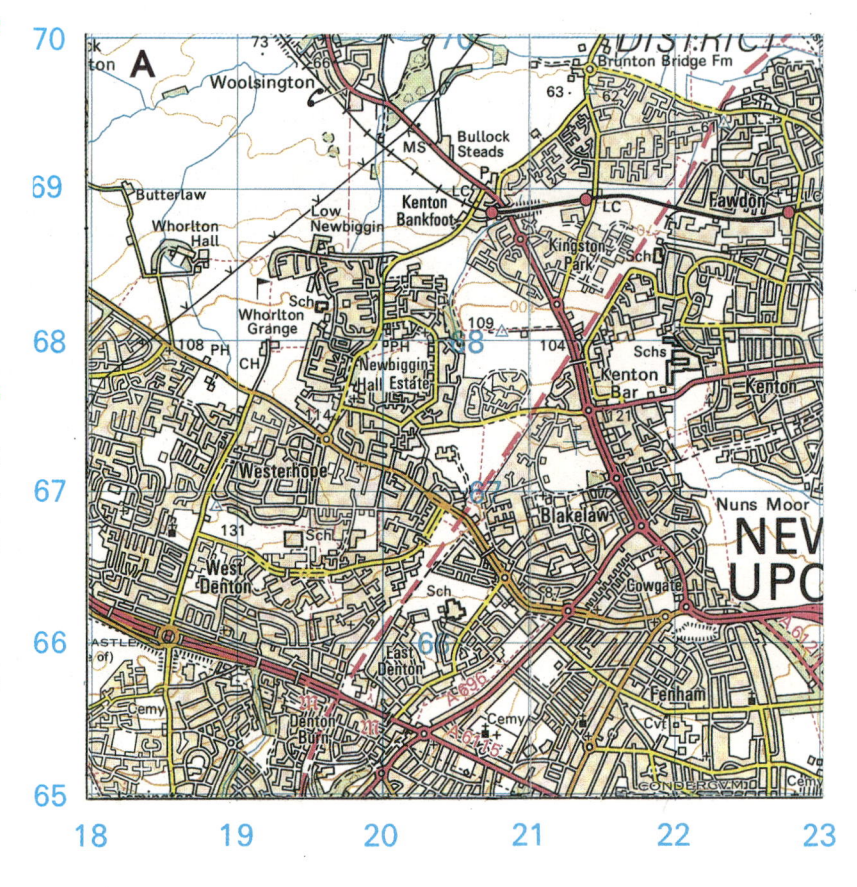

1:50 000 Ordnance Survey map extract

A is a part of an Ordnance Survey map which shows the area around the Newcastle superstore.

CORE ACTIVITIES

1 Westerhope is one of the places that people travel from to shop at the Tesco superstore.
   - Find Westerhope on the map, **A**.
   - Complete these directions from Westerhope to Tesco using the words at the end.
     From the road junction at 192 677, go south ____ as far as the roundabout at _____ where you turn onto a minor road. Keep going for about _____ until you reach the level crossing at Kenton _____. Turn right onto the main road and then left at the second _____, grid reference ____. The store will be on your ____ hand side.
     2 kilometres   213 683   Bankfoot   east   roundabout   right   196 674

2 Using Activity 1 as a guide:
   - Write directions to the superstore from:
     - Cowgate roundabout (221 662)
     - Whorlton Hall (188 686)

3 Look at **B**.
   - Why is the bus special?
   - How does the bus help Tesco make money?
   - The bus runs on Thursdays and Fridays only. Try to think of two reasons why those days should be chosen.

4 **C** is an artist's impression of the Tesco superstore.
   - Make a labelled sketch of **C** to show these features:
     single-storey building   flat site   car park   trees
   - Match each of the four features you have labelled with one of these statements about out of town superstores:
     - They are designed for people with cars.
     - Disabled people can move round them easily.
     - They pick land that is cheap to build on.
     - Landscaping is done to make them attractive.

Going Shopping

B

TESCO
Changing the way Britain Shops.

Catch a FREE bus to Tesco Kingston Park

C

TESCO
Changing the way Britain shops.

Tesco Superstore, Kingston Park, Newcastle

From Wednesday, 15th June, a brand new store for Kingston Park. A welcome change for you.

Tesco Superstore, Kingston Park, Newcastle-upon-Tyne

D

- "SMALL SHOPKEEPERS LIKE ME CAN'T COMPETE AGAINST THESE SUPERSTORES."
- "SUPERSTORES GIVE PEOPLE MORE CHOICE AT PRICES THEY CAN AFFORD — AND THEY DON'T GET WET BECAUSE IT'S ALL UNDER ONE ROOF."
- "IT'S MUCH EASIER, EVERYTHING GOES IN THE CAR SO THERE ARE NO HEAVY BAGS TO CARRY."
- "IT'S ALL RIGHT FOR PEOPLE WITH CARS. I CAN'T GET THERE VERY EASILY, AND I STILL HAVE BAGS TO CARRY."
- "I CAN DO ALL MY SHOPPING IN ONE SHOP."
- "THERE ISN'T AS MUCH CHOICE AS IN THE CITY CENTRE SHOPS. LITTLE SPECIALIST SHOPS ARE BETTER."

Different views

5 Out of town shopping is something which people have different views about, as **D** shows.
- Read **D** carefully.
- Make a table to show views for and against out town shopping places.

EXTENSION ACTIVITIES

6 For an out of town supermarket you know:
- Draw a labelled sketch to show its main features.
- Make a sketch map to show its accessibility.

7 Look at **B** and **C**. They are both pieces of advertising. They are made to make the superstore seem as good as possible.
- Why do you think Tesco did not use a photo of the superstore?
- How does the drawing make the shop look better? (*HINT*: Think about weather, size, number of cars, colours)

8.4 SHOPPING WITHOUT SHOPS

Target

* To understand that people can go shopping without going to shops.
* To learn something about the motorway network in Britain.

People can go shopping without going to shops. For example, some people do some of their shopping from home. They choose goods from a catalogue and have them delivered. One of these catalogues is called the Next Directory. Companies who send goods like this are often called mail order firms. The Next Directory company is based in Leicester. **A** shows where Leicester is, as well as where motorways are in Britain.

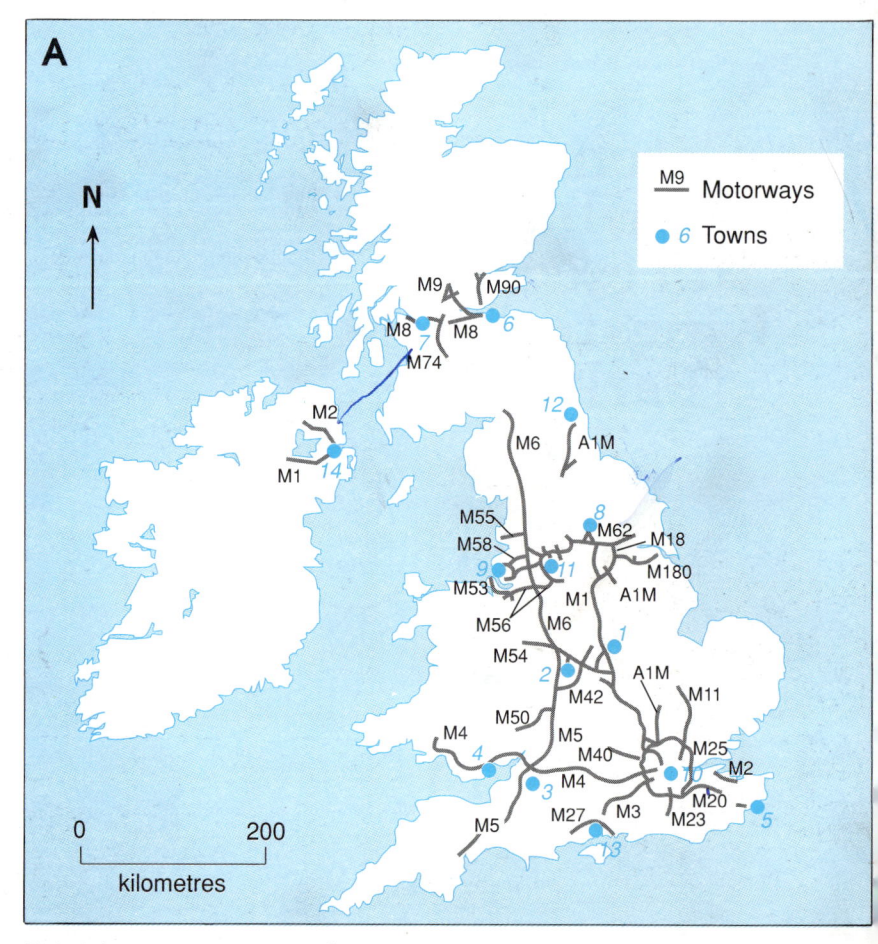

A

Britain's motorway network

CORE ACTIVITIES

1 **A** shows the location of Leicester and these other towns:
  Birmingham Bristol Cardiff Dover
  Edinburgh Glasgow Leeds Liverpool
  London Manchester Newcastle-upon-Tyne
  Southampton Belfast
  - Use an atlas to make a key for the 14 towns on the map.
  - List them one under the other.
  - Next to each town write down the motorway, or sometimes motorways, that serve it.
    EXAMPLE: Leicester = M1.

2 The Next Directory is based in Leicester.
  - Which motorways could be used to take goods to each of these places:
    - London
    - Glasgow
    - Southampton
    - Bristol
    - Manchester

3 The Next Directory promises to deliver goods in 48 hours if people telephone their order. It says it cannot do this for areas like the Isle of Man, the Isle of Wight and the Channel Islands.
  - Why do you think this is?
  - Write a sentence to explain what you think.

4 Look closely at **B**.
  - Use it to collect these facts:
    - the name of the building in the background
    - two types of goods being sold on the stalls
    - what the weather is like
      (*HINT*: Look at people's clothes)

5 Look back to **D** in Unit 8.2.
  - Find the market and write down the grid reference of the square it is in.
  - Draw a sketch map of the streets in that square and in the square to the north. You will need to make the squares larger than they are on the map.
  - On your map use colours or symbols and a key to show the pedestrianised streets.

80

Going Shopping

There is an open air market in Norwich six days a week. It is the largest in Europe.

Norwich market

Mail order shopping

6 Think about markets.
- Why do you think people shop in markets?
- Why are markets often in city centres rather than on the outskirts?

7 **C** shows the stages in ordering goods from a catalogue like the Next Directory. The pictures are not in any order.
- What order should they be in for the system to work? Either write the captions in a list to show the right order, or draw the pictures again so they follow on in the correct way.
- Why do you think companies like the Next Directory are called mail order companies?

EXTENSION ACTIVITIES

8 For a market you know:
- Make a list of different things the market sells.
- Draw a sketch map to show where it is located in the town.
- What day is the market held? Write a few sentences to describe what the town is like on market day.

9 Look again at the stages involved in mail order shopping.
- What group or groups of people do you think this will most appeal to? Why?
- What are your feelings about this type of shopping?

10 You will need a road atlas which shows motorways and main roads.
- How would a lorry reach your local town from Leicester?
- Write directions you would give the lorry driver. Include the roads to use, distances travelled and directions taken.

8.5 ACROSS THE CHANNEL

Target

* To look at shopping across the Channel.
* To investigate some of the effects of the Channel Tunnel.

The English Channel is the sea between the south coast of England and the north coast of France. Some people cross the Channel to go shopping. They only go sometimes to buy special things. Ferries are the transport they use. **A** shows some Sealink routes across the Channel, and their crossing times.

B shows part of the Sealink ferry company brochure. It is to persuade people to go shopping across the Channel.

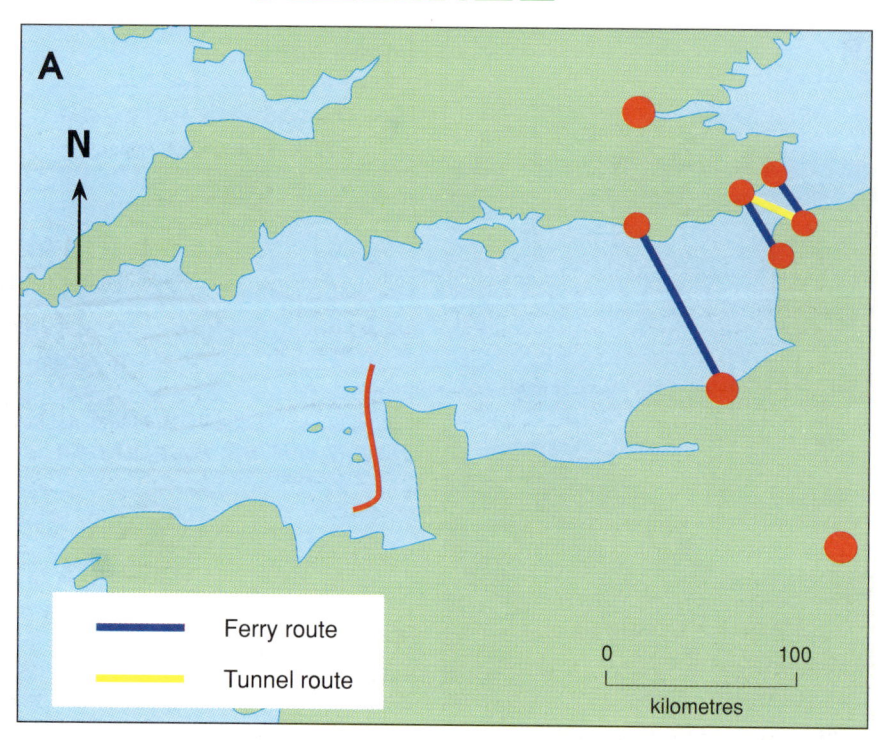

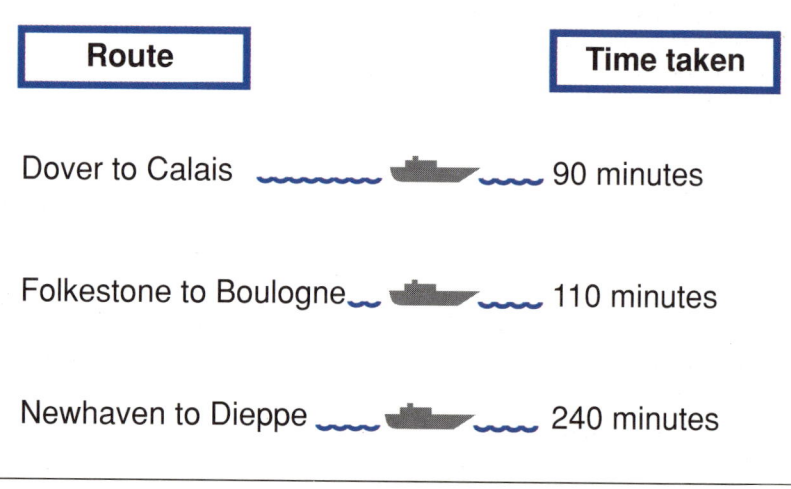

A

Ferry route
Tunnel route

Route	Time taken
Dover to Calais	90 minutes
Folkestone to Boulogne	110 minutes
Newhaven to Dieppe	240 minutes

Crossing the Channel

CORE ACTIVITIES

1 You will need a copy of the map, shown by **A**.
- With the help of an atlas, add these labels:
  France England English Channel Dover
  Folkestone Newhaven Boulogne Calais
  Dieppe London Paris
- Make a bar graph to show the sailing times of ferries on the three routes shown by **A**.
- What are the straight line distances for each of the three Sealink routes?
Use the scale in your atlas to help you find out.
- Record them in a table.
- Make a second bar graph to show them.

2 Study **B**.
- Copy this writing, and fill in the gaps using the words at the end:
Sealink says France is the land of ____ and _____ . It wants people to go shopping in the French towns of _____, _____ and _____ . The people in the photo are going shopping in a French _____ . In the writing from the brochure it says they could also go shopping in a _____ or on the _____ on the way back.
hypermarket Dieppe wine Boulogne romance market Calais ferry

82

Going Shopping

B

FRANCE
LAND OF WINE AND ROMANCE

SHOPPERS
FROM £42

CALAIS, BOULOGNE & DIEPPE

For a taste of France without going too far, choose from these three Channel Ports waiting to surprise you at the end of your crossing. Historical Dieppe, friendly Calais and Boulogne are more than just transit stops and ideal for a quick break.

Whichever you choose, you'll find that the French 'joie de vivre' starts at the water's edge.

Take a break with one night in an hotel, enjoy fine french cuisine in a wide choice of restaurants and bars, and shop in the hypermarkets for all the goodies you can't buy at home. Prices are unbeatable, but save some spending money for your duty-free shopping on the way back.

You'll be accommodated in a comfortable 2 star hotel with continental breakfast in a twin, double or 3 bedded room with ensuite bath or shower and wc.

Shopping à la française

Going shopping in France

The Channel Tunnel is due to open in 1993. Trains will run through the tunnel, and people will be able to load their cars onto the trains.

C shows the difference the Channel Tunnel is expected to make to journey times between Paris and London.

C

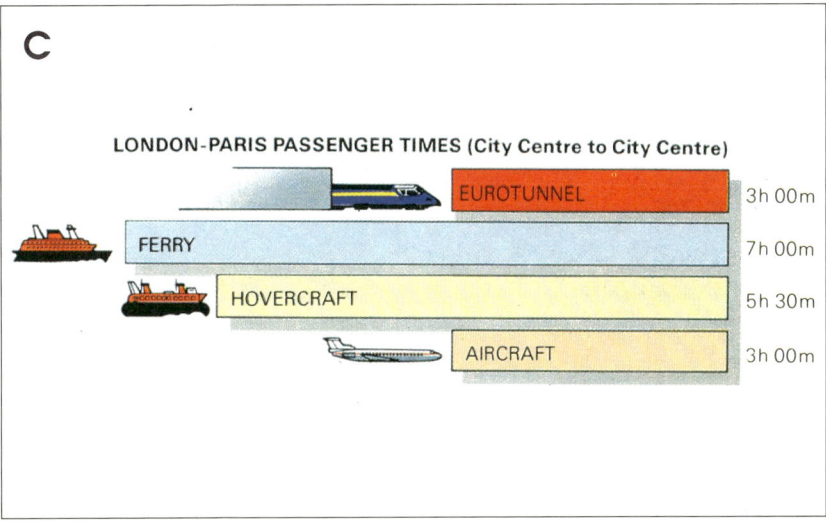

LONDON-PARIS PASSENGER TIMES (City Centre to City Centre)

EUROTUNNEL	3h 00m
FERRY	7h 00m
HOVERCRAFT	5h 30m
AIRCRAFT	3h 00m

Quicker by tunnel?

3 Sealink wants to make going shopping across the Channel sound good. **B** is advertising this fact.
- Write a sentence about each of the following, saying how the brochure makes them sound good:
  - France
  - Dieppe
  - Calais and Boulogne
  - French cuisine
  - shopping prices

4 Look at **C**.
- Use it to collect these data:
  - means of transport
  - journey time
  - time difference with tunnel crossing
- Put the data you have collected into a table.
- Make a bar graph to show how much longer other forms of transport take compared with the tunnel.

5 The actual Channel crossing part of a tunnel journey is expected to take 35 minutes.
- How many times quicker is that than the present ferry journey from Dover to Calais? Choose from these answers:
  about twice as quick
  about three times as quick
  about four times as quick

EXTENSION ACTIVITY

6 Building the Channel Tunnel has raised strong feelings.
- How would you expect the following groups of people to feel about it:
  - someone who works on a Sealink ferry
  - a family who live close to the tunnel entrance
  - the sales manager of a company wanting to **export** goods to Europe?

9.1 LEISURE TIME

Target

* To learn what leisure time is.
* To understand that people use leisure time in many different ways and that there are many different places for leisure.
* To read and make a **pie-chart**.

People work, rest and play. When they are not at work, and not asleep, they have spare time. This is called leisure time.

There are many ways to spend leisure time. Some people choose to be energetic and active, while others are quite happy to be inactive, simply passing the time and doing nothing in particular. Leisure time can be very active, like rock-climbing, or very passive, like sun-bathing.

Leisure time can also differ depending upon where it is spent. It can be, for example, be spent indoors or outdoors.

A

Leisure activities. How do you choose to spend your leisure time?

CORE ACTIVITIES

1 Look at **A**. It shows different ways in which leisure time can be spent.
   • Make a list of these.
   • Now split your list into two by deciding which of them you think are active and which you think are passive (inactive). You could make a table to show the two lists:

ACTIVE LEISURE TIME	PASSIVE LEISURE TIME

   • For each one in your list, write down the place where you would expect the activity to take place.
   EXAMPLE: Watching television = home.

2 Leisure activities can be inside, like playing computer games. They can also be outside, like jogging.
   • Make your own list of leisure activities together with the places where they might take place.

3 **B** shows Karen's time clock for one day.
   • Use it to complete these sentences:
   - Karen gets up at _____ .
   - She is at school from _____ to _____ .
   - Karen goes to bed at _____ .
   - The number of hours she is asleep is _____
   - She works for _____ hours a day.
   - She has _____ hours left.

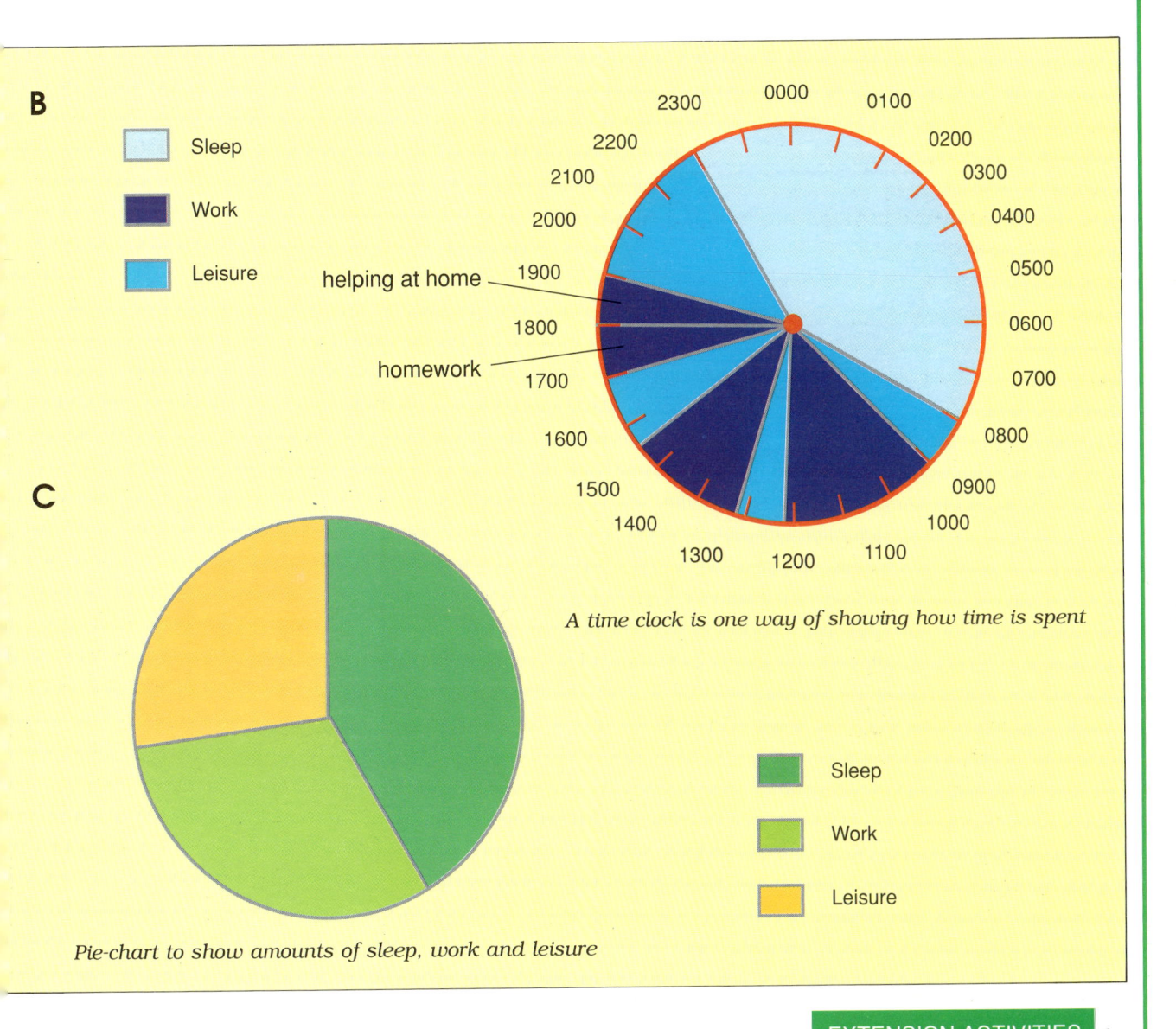

Places for Leisure

B

Sleep
Work
Leisure

helping at home
homework

A time clock is one way of showing how time is spent

C

Sleep
Work
Leisure

Pie-chart to show amounts of sleep, work and leisure

4 Karen's spare time is not all free to use as she wants. She has to get ready and go to school in the mornings so that takes up the time between 08.00 and 09.00.
- Write down another time period when her spare time has to be spent in a certain way.
- Draw your own time clock for one day.
- Make a table to show how many hours you work, how many hours you sleep and how many leisure hours you have in one day.

5 Look at **C**. Although it looks similar to **B** it is in fact a **pie-chart**. It can be used to compare the total amounts of time Karen sets aside for sleep, work and leisure.
- Using the information (Activity 4) draw a pie-chart to show the time you set aside for sleep, work and leisure.

EXTENSION ACTIVITIES

6 Keep a leisure diary for a week.
- For each day write down the leisure hours you have, what activities you do in them and what places you use.

7 Interview people about their leisure time.
- Ask them about their leisure activities and where they do them.
- Make time clocks to show their days.

9.2 LEISURE IN A TOWN - EXETER

Target

* To look at the location of leisure places in a city.

Exeter is a city in Devon and, like most cities, it has many different types of **leisure facilities.**

There are parks and open spaces as well as indoor leisure places, like sports centres and a cinema.

Most of these leisure facilities are in and around the city centre because that makes them easy for everyone to get to.

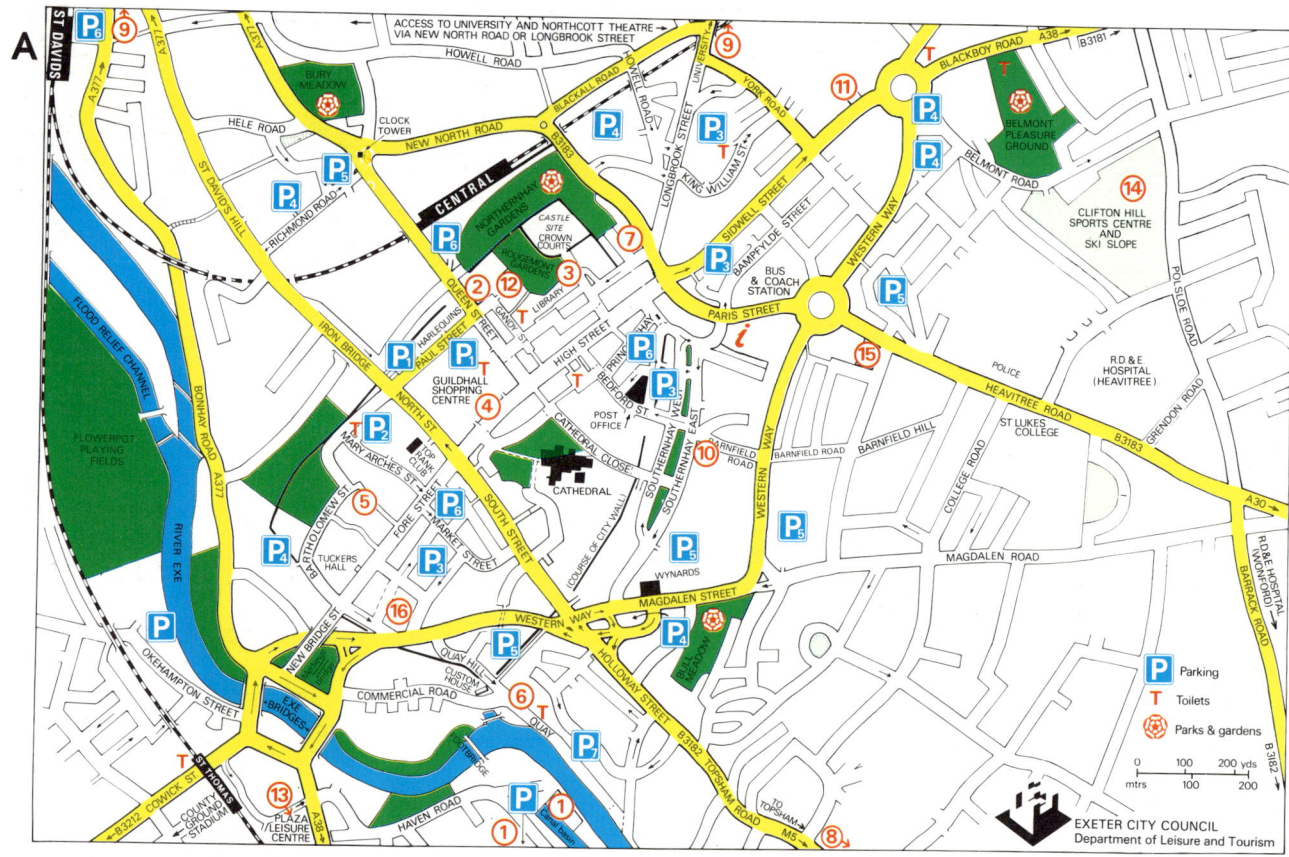

Exeter city centre. Why is this part of the city easy to reach?

1. Exeter Maritime Museum
2. Royal Albert Memorial Museum
3. Rougemont House Museum (Costume and Lace)
4. Guildhall
5. St. Nicholas Priory
6. Underground Passages
7. Quay House
8. Topsham Museum
9. Northcott Theatre
10. Barnfield Theatre
11. Odeon Cinema
12. Exeter and Devon Arts Centre
13. The Plaza
14. Clifton Hill Sports Centre
15. Swimming Pool and Fitness Centre
16. Spacex Gallery

Places for Leisure

B

The PLAZA

WAVES

It's summer all the year round at Waves, with tropical heat, exotic plants, waterfalls, a hot geyser – plus the thrills of the 50 metre water shute. The lagoon-shaped pool slopes gently to 2 metres and there's a special pool for parents and toddlers.
Then enjoy fun food at **CASCADES**. With burgers, fries, really thick milkshakes, coke – and unbelievable ice cream Sundaes – this is the ultimate poolside café and free viewing area for **WAVES**.

80° WHATEVER THE WEATHER!

You'll find something for everyone to do at The Plaza – and it can be as strenuous or as relaxing as you like.
PLAZASPORTS – Squash, Badminton – plus a total programme of indoor sports for all ages and all levels. The multi-purpose sports hall is the Best in the West.
BODYLINE – Fitness, bodycare and relaxation in ideal surroundings. The Spa Pool, Sauna, Steam Room, Sun Suite and fitness gym are open to day visitors.
MAINFRAME – The perfect atmosphere for Snooker, with nine full-sized tables and an intimate bar. Experts and beginners welcome.

The Plaza - Exeter's Pleasure Centre

CORE ACTIVITIES

1. Look at **A**. Suppose you wanted to travel into Exeter city centre to use its leisure facilities.
   - List three ways in which you could reach the city centre.

2. There are four parks and gardens shown on **A**.
   - Write out a list of their names.
   - How far is each one from the centre of the city? (*HINT*: Think of St. Peter's Cathedral as the centre)
   - What else can you say about their location?

3. The Plaza is known as Exeter's Pleasure Centre. It offers a wide range of indoor leisure activities.
   - Which number in the key is The Plaza?

4. Look again at **A**.
   - Describe the location of The Plaza in Exeter's city centre.
   - Which main road does it lie next to?

5. Using **A**:
   - Write directions for people who arrive at Exeter Central Station and want to walk to:
     - The Plaza
     - Clifton Hill Sports Centre
     - The Rougemont House Museum (Costume and Lace)
     - Barnfield Theatre
     - Spacex Gallery
     - Swimming pool and fitness centre
     - Royal Albert Memorial Museum

EXTENSION ACTIVITIES

6. Think about why people come to The Plaza.
   - Design an advertising poster for The Plaza to show people how good it is and get them to come. You might include these points:
     - it's tropical inside
     - it has its own car park
     - it is free to get in, you only pay for what you use

7. Find out about leisure places in your local town.
   - Make a list of them and make a map to show their locations.
   - Design a poster or brochure for one of these leisure places to show how good it is and how people can get there.

8. The City of Exeter is in a region which is often called the South West Peninsula.
   - Find out what peninsula means and write a definition.

9.3 DARTMOOR NATIONAL PARK

Target

* To learn that **National Parks** are parts of the countryside that are protected.
* To understand that people visit National Parks to enjoy them as leisure places.
* To test hypotheses.

Dartmoor is a hilly area of Devon which has been made a **National Park**. The National Park authorities aim to preserve the natural beauty of the area, as well as provide access for members of the public who come to enjoy its scenery.

A

A view over part of Dartmoor National Park

B

The 10 National Parks of Britain

CORE ACTIVITIES

1 Look at **A**.
- Copy and complete this description of the view. Use words from the list at the end to fill in the gaps. Across the dry _____ wall is a _____. In the distance are _____. In the centre is a small _____ with an historic _____. In one of the fields, _____ are grazing.
  village moor stone sheep church valley
- Make an outline sketch of **A** and label on it the features that you have just described.

2 **C** gives data about visitors to Dartmoor.
- Use these data to test these hypotheses:
  - Most people come to Dartmoor by car.
  - People travel hundreds of miles to visit Dartmoor.
  - Walking is the most popular activity for visitors to Dartmoor.
  - Most people walk at least 2 miles from their car.

Places for Leisure

Visitor data - supplied by The Dartmoor National Park and Devon County Council Traffic Survey.

C

Visitors to Dartmoor	%
- the transport used	
car	95
coach	3
bus, cycle, foot	2
- where they come from	
Plymouth	29
Torbay	23
Newton Abbott	6
Teignmouth/Dawlish	6
Exeter	7
rest of Devon	27
Cornwall	3
- what they come for	
walking	59
sightseeing	29
picnic	15
to visit cafes and shops	13
just to sit	10
to play games	6
climb	6
photography	3
to walk dogs	1
minority activities (e.g. pony trekking)	1
- how far they go from their car	
stay in car	18
up to 100 metres	25
up to 1 mile	32
1 - 2 miles	4
2 - 5 miles	18
5 - 10 miles	2
over 10 miles	1

Visitor data

3 Use **C** and Activity 2 to help you to answer these questions:
- What percentage of people do not use a car to reach Dartmoor?
- Which town is the biggest source of visitors to Dartmoor?
- What percentage of visitors come from Exeter?
- What percentage of people never leave their car?
- Out of every hundred visitors, how many do a minority activity, like pony trekking?

4 You will need an outline map of the British Isles.
Use **B** and your atlas to:
- Plot the 10 National Parks shown on **B**.
- Mark these cities:
  London Cardiff Newcastle-upon-Tyne Plymouth Bristol Manchester Leeds Liverpool Sheffield Middlesbrough
- Make a table to show the main city closest to each National Park.
- With the help of the scale in your atlas, find out the distance from London to each of the National Parks. Make a table to show the data you collect.

5 Look closely at the location of the 10 National Parks.
- Can you suggest why they are all in the north or west of Britain?

EXTENSION ACTIVITY

6 Think about the scenery of Dartmoor and about the land itself.
- Design a poster called 'Visit Dartmoor'. Use pictures to show what leisure activities people can do there.

89

9.4 PROTECTING THE COUNTRYSIDE

Target

* To have a look at the effects that visitors are having on National Parks.
* To see how visitors can help look after the countryside.

A

More and more people are visiting the countryside, including National Parks like Dartmoor. However, people often go to the most famous spots and miss other places.

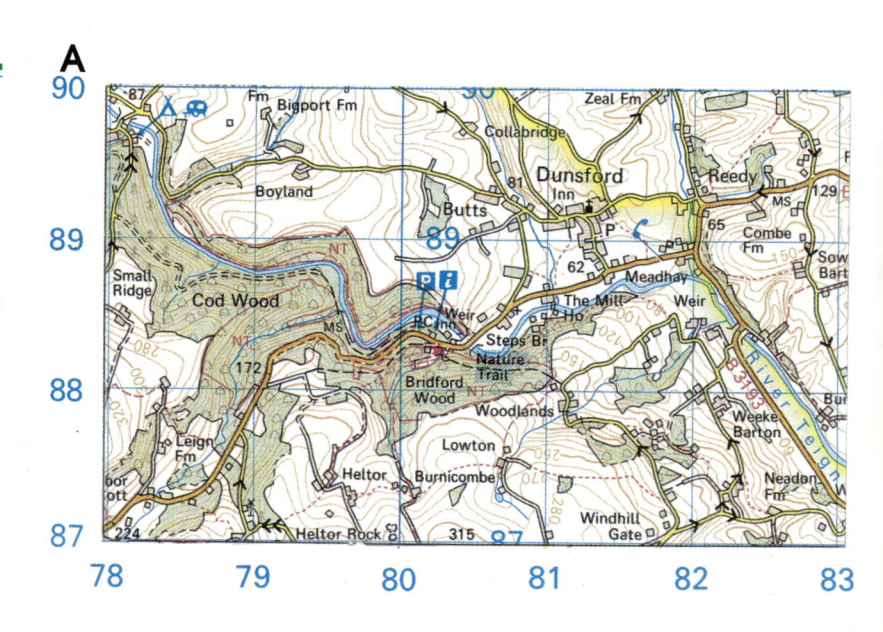

B

	Steps Bridge	New Bridge	Postbridge
1982	16 000	42 000	40 000
1983	13 000	35 000	50 000
1984	18 000	30 000	55 000
1985	20 000	31 000	55 000
1986	19 000	29 000	50 000
1987	19 000	29 000	53 000

Steps Bridge, New Bridge and Postbridge are popular places, within Dartmoor National Park, that attract a lot of visitors.

Places that attract a lot of visitors like this are called **'honeypots'**, because the visitors are like bees swarming around a pot of honey.

CORE ACTIVITIES

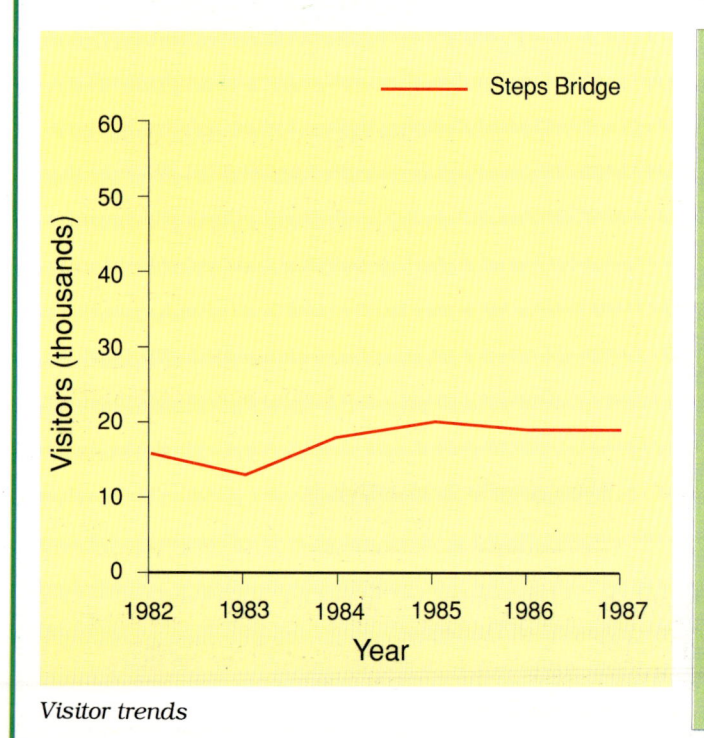

1 Using the O.S. map extract:
● Find Steps Bridge (804 883)
● Complete the following description of its tourist attractions. The missing words are at the end of the description.
   Steps Bridge is surrounded by woods owned by the _____ _____. There is a _____ trail. For day visitors there is a car _____, public _____ and a tourist _____ centre. People can stay at the _____, or the _____ or _____ site or in the _____ hostel.
   park inn caravan National Trust conveniences nature camp youth information
● Give the straight line distances and compass directions from Steps Bridge to each of these places:
   - Combe Farm (828 890)
   - Windhill Gate (817 871)
   - Campsite at Boyland (782 897)

Visitor trends

Places for Leisure

C

Honeypot problems

When a 'honeypot' site has too many visitors, problems can result. Large numbers of visitors passing over the same spot can damage the site through over-use. Sometimes, facilities are built specially for visitors and these can spoil the area if they are not carefully planned.
People visiting the country should treat it carefully so that others can enjoy it too.

D

When in the country please follow the Country Code:
- respect its life and work
- guard against all risk of fire
- fasten all gates
- keep your dogs under close control
- keep to public footpaths across farmland
- use gates and stiles to cross walls etc.
- leave livestock, crops and machinery alone
- take your litter home
- help to keep all water clean
- protect wildlife, plants and trees
- take care on country roads
- make no unnecessary noise

The Country Code

2 Look at **B** and at this list:
 - Steps Bridge 53 000.
 - New Bridge 19 000.
 - Postbridge 29 000.
- The wrong number of visitors has been put next to each place. Rewrite the list, with the correct numbers next to each place.

3 Think about the facts you collected for your answers to Activity 1.
- Use these facts to write at least three sentences describing why so many people visit each of the three places shown in **B**.

4 **B** also shows a line graph.
- Make your own graph to show similar lines for visitors to New Bridge and Postbridge. (HINT: Use a different colour for each line and remember to show a key)

5 Line graphs show trends.
- Read this description of the line graph for Steps Bridge: "The trend for Steps Bridge is going up, though there was a fall in 1983".
- Write your own sentences to describe the trends for New Bridge and for Postbridge.

EXTENSION ACTIVITIES

6 **D** shows The Country Code.
- Use it to draw a series of cartoons to show some rules from the Country Code.
- Write out the rules which have been broken by people in **C**.

7 Think about a place you know that has been spoiled by people not treating it properly. Your local playground or park might be an example.
- Draw a labelled sketch to show the damage that has been done.
- Write a few sentences to say how people should have behaved.

9.5 SUN, SEA AND SAND

Target

* To understand why many people take sun, sea and sand holidays in Mediterranean countries like Italy.
* To plan a trip to the Mediterranean.

Sun, sea and sand are what many people seek when they plan their holiday. Every year millions of people flock to the countries around the Mediterranean Sea, for their holidays.

The Italian resort of Cattolica is one place where holidaymakers can find these special three S's. Here, the summer climate is hot and reliable with very little rain.

The Adriatic Riviera is the stretch of Italy's coastline where Cattolica is located. The main airport for the region is at Rimini.

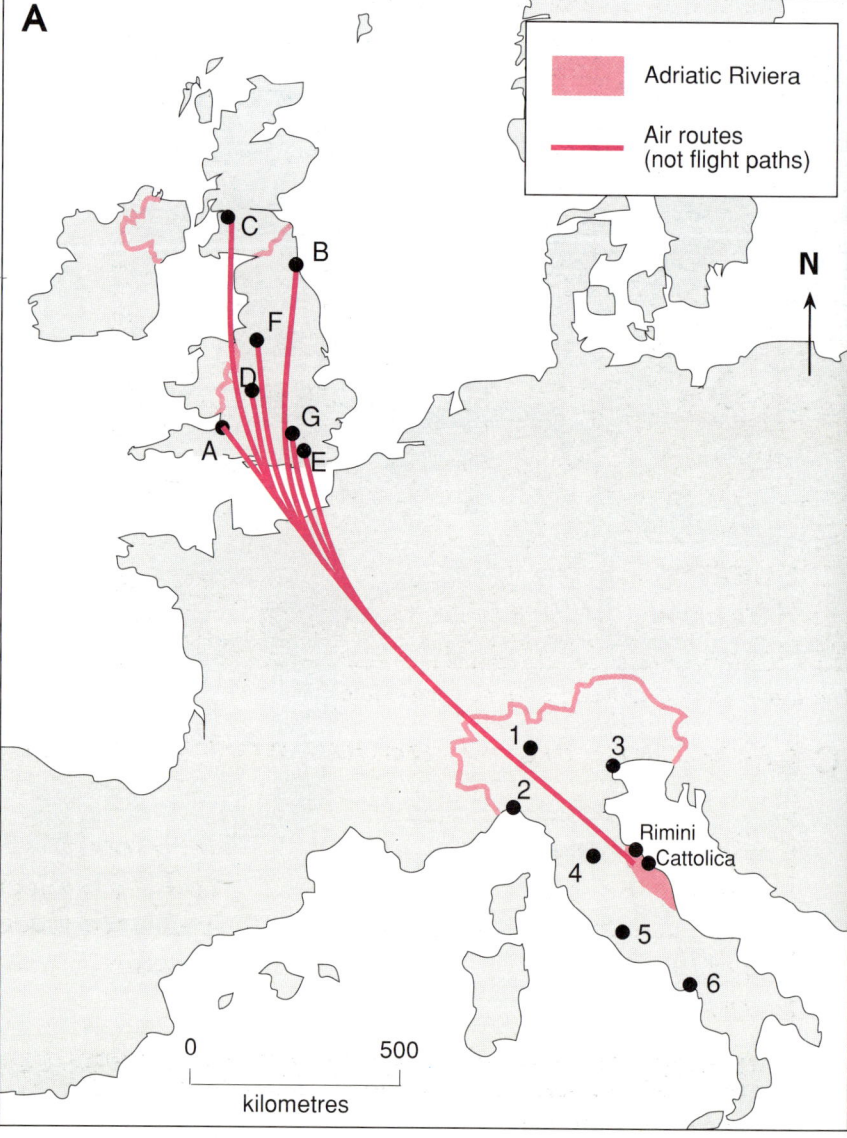

A

Routes to the sun

CORE ACTIVITIES

1 Using **A** and an atlas:
   • Make a sketch map of Italy showing where the Adriatic Riviera is.
   • Make a key to show the names of cities 1 to 6.
   • Add these labels:
     Mediterranean Sea   Adriatic Sea   Sardinia   Sicily

2 **A** shows the locations of seven airports in Britain.
   • With the help of an atlas, make a key to show their names. These are the names you are looking for:
     London–Gatwick   Luton   Bristol   Manchester   Glasgow   Birmingham   Newcastle-Upon-Tyne

3 Holidaymakers going to Cattolica arrive first at Rimini airport.
   • How far is Cattolica from Rimini? Use the map scale to find out.

4 People staying in Cattolica can go on day trips to other places including Rome and Venice.
   • Write down the straight line distances and directions from Cattolica to both of these places.

5 Look at the photo in **B**.
   • With its help, make a list of leisure activities people can do on beaches. You should write down at least six, but try to make a really long list.

92

Places for Leisure

B is a photo of Cattolica's beach. It also gives some more details about the resort, including a comparison with London of how many hours of sunshine a day usually has in each summer month.

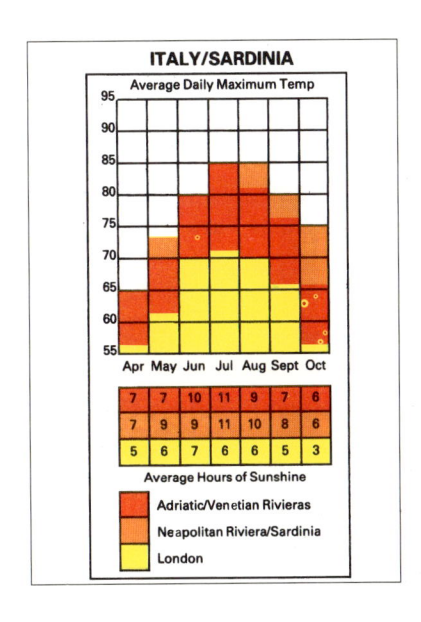

B

The three S's of Cattolica - sun, sea and sand

ITALY/SARDINIA
Average Daily Maximum Temp

	Apr	May	Jun	Jul	Aug	Sept	Oct
	7	7	10	11	9	7	6
	7	9	9	11	10	8	6
	5	6	7	6	6	5	3

Average Hours of Sunshine

- Adriatic/Venetian Rivieras
- Neapolitan Riviera/Sardinia
- London

C

Plenty of sun
Sandy beach
Blue sea to swim in safely
Lots of fun
Modern hotels

Pretty resort
Plenty of nightlife
Good eating places
Dancing

Karen's holiday checklist

6 Using the data about sunshine hours in **B**:
- Make bar graphs for the Adriatic Riviera and for London.
- Make a new table to show the difference in daily sunshine hours between Cattolica and London from April to October.

7 Read what **B** says about Cattolica.
- Compare it with the checklist of what Karen is looking for in a holiday (**C**).
- Copy **C** and put ticks against the things you can find in **B**.

8 It looks as though Cattolica would suit Karen.
- Would it suit you?
Write a few sentences to explain why it would or why it would not. (*HINT*: You might like to make your own holiday checklist to help you decide)

EXTENSION ACTIVITY

9 Try to obtain a travel brochure.
- Find out about a holiday in a seaside resort in another country.
- Draw a sketch map to show where it is.
- Describe the journey you would have to make to get there from your home.
- What attractions does the resort have. Make a checklist.
- Draw a graph to show how much sun it receives.

93

GLOSSARY

A Access	the ability to reach a place	7.4
Aerial photography	taking photos from the air	5.2
Arable farm	farm which grows crops	6.5
B Bar graph	a graph using columns	1.3
Barrage	a barrier built by people to hold water back	5.4
Business Park	an area specially planned for businesses	7.3
C Capital	the main city in a country, where the government is based	4.5
Central Business District	the office and shopping area of a town or city centre	3.4
City	a very large town	2.1
Climate	average weather conditions	6.5
Commuter	someone who travels into a city every day to work	6.4
Consumer	a person who buys goods and services for their own needs	7.5
Contour line	a line on a map joining places which are the same height above sea level	3.4
Conurbation	a large built-up area made up of settlements which have joined together	2.1
D Dairy farm	farm that produces milk and milk products	6.5
Data	collected facts	1.3
Decay	areas or property that are run-down	4.2
Divided bar graph	a bar, split into sections which shows how something is shared out	6.4
E EC	European Community	4.5
Environment	our surroundings	4.3
Export	to sell goods abroad	8.5
F Factors	things which need to be considered	6.3
Farmstead	a settlement of one farm	2.1
Fresh water lake	a lake that is not salty	5.4
G Geography	the study of places, people and their environments	1.1
Goods	items which are made and sold	6.1
Green Belt	a band of protected countryside around a city	4.3
Grid	a set of squares drawn on a map	2.3
Grid references	grid line numbers	2.3
H Hamlet	a small settlement without a church, usually just a few houses	2.1

	Heavy industry	a business which makes heavy goods	7.5
	Hill farm	farm which specialises in raising sheep	6.5
	Honeypot	a site, such as a beauty spot, which attracts lots of visitors	9.4
	Hypothesis	an idea which can be tested	3.2
I	Industrial	an area where there are factories and warehouses	3.4
	Inner city	parts of a city close to the centre	4.2
	Inputs	anything which goes into a system	6.2
	Issue	something which people have different views about	1.5
	Industrial estate	a place where factories and warehouses are grouped together	7.5
K	Key	it explains what the symbols on a map mean	1.1
L	Labour	the people who work for a business	7.4
	Land-use zones	areas where the land is mostly used for the same purpose	3.4
	Leisure	free time	4.4
	Light industry	a business which makes light goods	7.5
	Line graph	a graph using a line to show how something has changed	4.1
	Links	something joining two places, for example, a road	2.4
	Locations	where places are	2.5
	Leisure facilities	something which is provided for people's leisure activities	9.2
M	Manufacturing industries	businesses which make goods	7.3
	Map	a drawing which shows part of the earth's surface	2.3
	Market garden	farm which specialises in growing vegetables and fruit	6.5
	Market town	a town which has or used to have a market	3.5
N	National Park	an area of special countryside which is protected for people to enjoy	9.3
	Neighbourhood	the small area around people's homes	4.4
	New Town	a town which has been planned and newly built	4.4
O	One-way traffic system	streets which allow traffic movement in only one direction	3.3
	Open space	land which is not built on	4.1
	Ordnance Survey map	the official organisation for making maps of UK	2.3
	Outputs	anything which comes out of a system	6.2
P	Pie-chart	a diagram which shows how something is shared, by slicing a circle	9.1

	Plan	a detailed map or drawing	1.2
	Pollution	harmful substances	4.2
	Population	the number of people who live in a place	4.4
	Profit	the money which has been earned by a business after all its costs have been paid	6.2
R	**Residential**	parts of a town or city where people live	3.4
	Rural	to do with the countryside	5.1
S	**Scale**	how many times a map or plan is smaller than the real world	1.5
	Services	businesses which help people	2.2
	Settlement	a place where people live	2.1
	Sketch map	a map drawn quickly and not to scale	1.1
	Spot height	a mark on a map showing the height of the land	3.4
	Street furniture	things in the street which are not buildings and do not move, e.g. lamp-posts	1.1
	Street survey	collecting and recording data	1.2
	Symbols	signs on a map	1.1
	System	an organised way to do something	6.2
	Systems diagram	a diagram to show how a system works	6.2
T	**Tally chart**	a table used to keep score	3.2
	Town	a settlement which has more services than a village, with shops, offices and factories and often a market	2.1
	Triangulation pillar	a pillar that marks the exact height of the land	3.4
	Trunk road	a main road of national importance	2.3
U	**Urban**	anything to do with towns and cities	5.1
	Urban area	somewhere that is built-up	4.3
	Urban decay	urban areas that are run-down	5.1
	Urban growth	the growing of cities and towns	4.5
	Urban renewal	the rebuilding of parts of urban areas	5.3
V	**Village**	a small settlement with a church and usually just a few services	2.1